"The Peace Corps was President John F. Kennedy's masterstroke of statecraft. I would never have gotten a higher education or been elected President of Peru had it not been for the Peace Corps, whose Volunteers worked throughout our country in the Sixties.

"This fast-paced memoir, *JFK & RFK Made Me Do It: 1960-1968*, highlights the gritty and consequential work Volunteers performed in rural and urban locales, including the three Volunteers who personally helped me break out of the cycle of poverty and gross discrimination that oppressed so many Indigenous people in my country.

"The author meticulously retraces Senator Robert Kennedy's triumphant trip through South America in November 1965, showing the enthusiastic support for JFK's Latin American strategy of a 'peaceful revolution,' while uncovering truths about those who worked to undermine it.

"I strongly recommend this extraordinary book. Written by a person who has lived on the ground in the Andes, trying to help the poor, his candid story exemplifies JFK's grass-roots vision for achieving peace. This book is a must-read for believers in equal opportunity and the power of higher education."

ALEJANDRO TOLEDO PH.D., President of Peru 2001-2006, author of *New York Times* bestseller, *The Shared Society*, 2015 Stanford University, translated into 10 languages. His newest: *Education & The Future of Latin America*, 2021, Lynne Rienner Publisher, Boulder, Colorado.

"The costs of peace are nothing compared to the costs of war, a fact that President John F. Kennedy knew well and used as the basis for his June 10, 1963 'strategy of peace' speech. In his insightful well-documented book, Sweet William uses JFK's Commencement Address to graduates of American University as the jumping-off point for his story of the quest for peace in The Sixties.

"Fifty-eight years later that speech remains a succinct roadmap to world peace. Every line of JFK's carefully thought-out speech is a step on the path to a world free of nuclear weapons. There's no better guide.

"Particularly inspiring is the book's emphasis on the important role public higher education plays in society, whether you're a Native American of Peru or a railroad switchman from San Berdoo.

"I had mixed feelings learning that so many of my classmates from UCLA were involved in Robert Kennedy's 1968 campaign to end the war that I was so actively engaged in. This book does a great job at showing the schizophrenic nature of the times, the elusiveness of peace."

CAPTAIN KENT W. EWING, US NAVY, RETIRED, Commanding Officer, USS AMERICA CV-66 (aircraft carrier) 1991 Gulf War: 444 sorties; Vietnam War fighter pilot; Fellow, Society of Experimental Test Pilots.

"My favorite part of Sweet William's memoir about the Sixties is Frank Mankiewicz and Myrna Loy discussing when Hollywood made its greatest movies, their list of the best, and why Hollywood stopped making them."

> JACK EPSTEIN, National/Foreign wire editor, *San Francisco Chronicle;* PCV Brazil 1968-1969, Panama 1969-1970; author, *Along the Gringo Trail,* And/Or Press, Berkeley CA 1977.

"A moving account of idealism, civic action and the crushing of hope in the 1960s, especially from Robert Kennedy's visit to Peru in 1965 to his murder in 1968. A reminder that peace is possible — and that the price of peace can be high."

> JAMES K. GALBRAITH, PH.D., The University of Texas at Austin

"Welcome and useful addition to the RFK saga."

> JULES WITCOVER, Washington journalist, columnist and author: *85 Days: The Last Campaign of Robert Kennedy,* Putnam Publications Group, 1969; *The Year The Dream Died: Revisiting 1968 in America,* Grand Central Publishing, 1998; *The American Vice Presidency: From Irrelevance to Power,* Smithsonian, 2014.

"Sweet William's memoir is nothing short of a captivating transnational history. The book shows how Peace Corps Volunteers developed a social life of their own that is usually ignored by classic diplomatic histories. These men and women developed friendships, established families, and came to know Peruvian society in a far more intimate way than they would ever have imagined.

"Their actions also show the challenges that the Alliance for Progress faced on the ground. Nowhere was this more evident than in the Mantaro Valley Rural Electric Cooperative in the Central Andes, one of Latin America's most ambitious electrification endeavors, where volunteers such as Sweet William not only had to earn the trust of indigenous Peruvians, but also fight for the support of their own government. No doubt this book will find a wide Peruvian audience, as the political history of the 1960s has not been widely studied or has been plagued by misconceptions. An essential text for those interested in Peru's — and thus Latin America's — Cold War."

GONZALO ROMERO SOMMER PH.D. , Pontificia Universidad Católica del Perú; author, *Alternating Currents: Political and Hydroelectric Power in Peru: 1895-1975,* Stony Brook University New York 2021.

"JFK's idealistic call to serve in the Peace Corps changed the trajectory of a railroad switchman's life.

"Author Sweet William tells the story of the Peace Corps adventures of his and his wife Marie, both recent UCLA graduates, as they embarked on their 'low budget honeymoon into the Andes.'

"Assigned to serve in the rural highlands of Peru, they crossed paths with Robert Kennedy, who after being elected U.S. Senator for New York, visited Peru on a fact-finding mission for his brother's revolutionary aid program for Latin America — the Alliance for Progress. What RFK discovered in Cusco is one of many revelations of American politics this book has to offer.

"Returning to LA after their Peace Corps service, the author and his wife became involved in local anti-war activities, and eventually joined RFK's run for the Presidency, actively supporting his plan to immediately end the Vietnam War.

"*JFK & RFK Made Me Do It: 1960-1968* is a richly detailed retelling of the Sixties from the unique perspective of Returned Peace Corps Volunteers. It is a tale of American idealism and how the Peace Corps is central to the aspiration for a world of peace."

> GLENN BLUMHORST, President & CEO, National Peace Corps Association, 2013-present; Managing Director, ACDI/VOCA – an international development nonprofit (18 years); PCV Guatemala 1988-91; licensed pilot.

". . . Peace Corps Volunteers have to learn peace, to live peace, and to labor for peace from the beginning of their service to the end of their days."

> BILL MOYERS, Peace Corps' founding Deputy Director; Special Assistant to President Johnson. Journalist: NBC, CBS, PBS News. Books: *Joseph Campbell and The Power of Myth*, Anchor, 1991; *Healing and the Mind,* Doubleday, 1993; *The Language of Life: A Festival of Poets,* Doubleday, 1995; *Moyers on America: A Journalist and His Times*, The New Press, 2004; *Moyers on Democracy,* Doubleday, 2008; *Bill Moyers Journal: The Conversation Continues*, The New Press, 2011. Awards: 36 Emmys, and a Lifetime Peabody Award.

JFK & RFK Made Me Do It
1960 –1968

ALSO BY SWEET WILLIAM

Venice of America: The American Dream Come True, 1976

"Flower power philosophy . . . a freeway to happiness."
— *Los Angeles Times* reviewer Rochelle Reed

JFK & RFK Made Me Do It
1960–1968

Sweet William

PEACE CORPS WRITERS

&

Constitutional Capers

JFK & RFK MADE ME DO IT: 1960–68

A Peace Corps Writers Book — an imprint of Peace Corps Worldwide

Copyright © 2021 by Sweet William

All rights reserved.

Printed in the United States of America

by Peace Corps Writers of Oakland, California.

No part of this book may be used or reproduced in any manner whatsoever without written permission except in the case of brief quotations contained in critical articles or reviews.

For more information, contact peacecorpsworldwide@gmail.com.

Peace Corps Writers and the Peace Corps Writers colophon are trademarks of PeaceCorpsWorldwide.org.

Edit and design: Marian Haley Beil

ISBN-13: 978-1-950444-09-0

Library of Congress Control Number: 2021913614

First Peace Corps Writers Edition, August 2021

When the power of love
overcomes the love of power,
the world will know peace.
— *Jimi Hendrix*

TABLE OF CONTENTS

>

JFK & RFK Made Me Do It

1960–1968

1

A STRATEGY OF PEACE

In the summer of 1961 I answered JFK's call to join the New Frontier. I was going to "begin anew" in the big city. I had severed my ties with the Citrus Belt — transferred my Santa Fe railroad seniority to the Los Angeles yards, and my academic credits from tiny UC Riverside to star-studded UCLA.

Graduation Day, June 11, 1963, was a day of working-class jubilation for me. I was the only railroad switchman to graduate from UCLA that day. Even if you included all six of the University of California campuses, I probably was the only blue-collar worker to receive a Bachelor of Arts degree.

Attending public institutions of higher learning at $75 a semester was the ultimate benefit of being an American. Few workers, though, realized how much higher education affected one's personal reality. It was an aphrodisiac for the mind that opened up doors one never knew existed.

The day before, on the east coast, President John Fitzgerald Kennedy announced in his commencement address to graduates of American University, his bold strategy for world peace and the curbing of the nuclear weapons race.

After battling through two Cuban Crises — the Bay of Pigs in 1961, and the Soviet Missile Crisis of 1962 — both of which had taken the world to the brink of thermonuclear war, President Kennedy was finally pushing his New Frontier agenda for world peace. He and Russian Premier Nikita Khrushchev had gone to the brink in October of 1962, and they definitely did not want to again face the horrible prospect of a nuclear exchange where tens of millions would perish. JFK was changing the focus of American foreign policy from war to peace.

As a World War II naval combat veteran, JFK knew that far more warriors wanted peace rather than war. As for me, having been born into that war, I had been raised all my life to be a warrior, to defend America against all enemies. But after enduring years of post-WWII warmongering, of terrifying hydrogen bomb testing, and of countless nuclear blasts in our own backyard of Las Vegas, JFK's 180-degree pivot toward peace felt like a graduation present. A world of peace would open up a whole new line of career opportunities for obsolete warriors.

What JFK said to graduates of American University affected me, a simple railroad switchman, for the rest of my life:

> I HAVE CHOSEN this time and this place to discuss a topic on which ignorance too often abounds and the truth is too rarely perceived; yet it is the most important topic on earth: world peace.
>
> What kind of peace do I mean? Not the peace of the grave or the security of the slave. I am talking about genuine peace, the kind of peace that makes life on earth worth living, the kind that enables men and nations to grow and to hope and to build a better life for their children — not merely peace for Americans, but peace for all men and women, not merely peace in our time but peace for all time.
>
> I speak of peace because . . . total war makes no sense in an age when great powers can maintain large and relatively invulnerable nuclear forces and refuse to surrender without resort to those forces . . . .. It makes no sense in an age when the deadly poisons produced by a nuclear exchange would be carried by wind and water and soil and seed to the far corners of the globe and to generations yet unborn.
>
> Today the expenditure of billions of dollars every year on weapons acquired for the purpose of making sure we never need to use them is essential to keeping the peace. But surely the acquisition of such idle stock-

piles — which can only destroy and never create — is not the only, much less the most efficient, means of assuring peace.

I speak of peace, therefore, as the necessary rational end of rational men . . .. Every thoughtful citizen who despairs of war and wishes to bring peace should begin by looking inward — by examining his own attitude toward the possibilities of peace, toward the Soviet Union, toward the course of the Cold War, and toward freedom and peace at home.

Let us examine our attitude toward peace itself . . . too many of us think it is impossible . . .. But that is a dangerous, defeatist belief. It leads to the conclusion that war is inevitable, that mankind is doomed — that we are gripped by forces we cannot control . . ..

Our problems are man-made — therefore, they can be solved by man . . .. Genuine peace must be the product of many nations, the sum of many acts. It must be dynamic, not static, changing to meet the challenge of each new generation. For peace is a process — a way of solving problems . . ..

World peace like community peace does not require that each man love his neighbor — it requires only that they live together in mutual tolerance — submitting their disputes to a just and peaceful settlement. Peace need not be impractical, and war need not be inevitable.

Among the many traits the peoples of the United States and the Soviet Union have in common, none is stronger than our abhorrence of war . . .. Should total war ever break out again our two countries would become the primary targets. It is an ironic but accurate fact that the two strongest powers are the two in the most danger of devastation . . .. Our two countries bear the heaviest burdens for we are both devoting massive sums of money on weapons that could be better devoted to combating ignorance, poverty and disease.

We are both caught up in a vicious and dangerous cycle in which suspicion on one side breeds suspicion on the other, and new weapons beget counter-weapons.

In short both [sides] have a mutually deep interest in a just and genuine peace and in halting the arms race . . .. If we cannot end now our differences, at least we can help make the world safe for diversity. In the final analysis, our most basic common link is that we all inhabit this small planet. We all breathe the same air. We all cherish our children's future. And we are all mortal.

In the search for peace . . . we must conduct our affairs in such a way that it becomes in the Communists' interest to agree on a genuine peace. Above all . . . nuclear powers must avert those confrontations, which bring an adversary to a choice of either a humiliating retreat or a nuclear war. To adopt that kind of course in the nuclear age would be evidence only of the bankruptcy of our policy — or of a collective death wish for the world.

We can seek a relaxation of tension without relaxing our guard . . .. We are unwilling to impose our system on any unwilling people — but we are willing and able to engage in peaceful competition with any people on earth.

We seek to strengthen the United Nations . . . to make it a more effective instrument for peace, to develop it into a genuine world security system — a system capable of resolving disputes on the basis of law, of insuring the security of the large and the small, and of creating conditions under which arms can finally be abolished . . .. It is our hope — and the purpose of allied policies — to convince the Soviet Union that she, too, should let each nation choose its own future, so long as that choice does not interfere with the choices of others. The Communist drive to impose their political and economic system on others is the primary cause of world tension today. For there can be no doubt that, if all the nations could refrain from interfering in the self-determination of others, the peace would be much more assured . . . .

We have also been talking in Geneva about the other first-step measures of arms control designed to limit the intensity of the arms race and to reduce the risks of accidental war. Our primary long-range interest in Geneva, however, is general and complete disarmament designed to take place by stages, permitting parallel political developments to build the new institutions of peace, which would take the place of arms . . . .. We intend to continue this effort in order that all countries, including our own, can better grasp what the problem and possibilities of disarmament are.

One major area of these negotiations . . . is in a treaty to outlaw nuclear tests. The conclusion of such a treaty . . . would check the spiraling arms race in one of its most dangerous areas. It would place the nuclear powers in a position to deal more effectively with one of the greatest hazards which man faces in 1963, the further spread of nuclear arms. It would increase our security and decrease the prospects for war . . . .

I am taking this opportunity, therefore, to announce two important decisions in this regard: First, Chairman Khrushchev, Prime Minister Macmillan, and I have agreed that high-level discussions will shortly begin in Moscow looking toward early agreement on a comprehensive test ban treaty.

Second, to make clear our good faith . . . I now declare that the United States does not propose to conduct nuclear tests in the atmosphere so long as other states do not do so. We will not be the first to resume. Such a declaration is no substitute for a formal binding treaty but I hope it will help us achieve one. Nor would such a treaty be a substitute for disarmament, but I hope it will help us achieve it.

Finally, my fellow Americans, let us examine our attitude toward peace and freedom here at home. The quality and spirit of our own society must justify and support our efforts abroad. We must show it in the dedication of our own lives — as many of you who are graduating today will have a unique opportunity to do, by serving without pay in the Peace Corps abroad or in the proposed National Service Corps here at home.

But wherever we are, we must all, in our daily lives, live up to the age-old faith that peace and freedom walk together. In too many of our cities today, the peace is not secure because the freedom is incomplete . . .. It is the responsibility of all citizens in all sections of this country to respect the rights of all others and to re-spect the law of the land . . ..

Is not peace, in the last analysis, basically a matter of human rights — the right to live out our lives without fear of devastation — the right to breathe air as na-ture provided it — the right of future generations to a healthy existence?

While we proceed to safeguard our national interests, let us also safeguard human interests. And the elimina-tion of war and arms is clearly in the interest of both. No treaty can provide absolute security against the risks of deception and evasion. But it can offer far more secu-rity and far fewer risks than an unabated, uncontrolled, unpredictable arms race.

The United States, as the world knows, will never start a war . . .. We shall be prepared if others wish it. We shall be alert to try to stop it. We shall also do our part to build a world of peace where the weak are safe and the strong are just. We are not helpless before that task or hopeless of its success. Confident and unafraid, we labor on — not toward a strategy of annihilation but toward a strategy of peace.

My fiancé Marie, who was a junior at UCLA, and I couldn't believe that peace was at hand. Immediately we sent in our applications for joining the Peace Corps, available to serve as Volunteers the following summer of 1964. Knowing some Spanish, we chose to be assigned to Latin America. Now, as the country began to move its focus away from war, there would be a need for experienced peacemakers to replace the warrior class.

Following graduation, I moved to downtown L.A. to be closer to the Santa Fe rail yards and its sooty, but superior, union wages. The sales and banking jobs offered a UCLA graduate with a Bachelor's degree earned only half of what I earned as a railroad switchman, so I continued working for the Santa Fe to get out of debt. Next June, as soon as Marie graduated, we would get married.

Three times a day — morning, swing and midnights — the Santa Fe yardmaster's office, located under the 1st Street Bridge on the west side of the L.A. River, filled needed eight-hour jobs from the Extra Board, selecting men by their seniority. Summer vacation always resulted in a higher demand for switchmen and my June 1957 seniority date allowed me to quickly reduce my graduation debts by working six and seven shifts a week.

The New Frontier that JFK had promised, in his July 15, 1960 Acceptance Speech in Los Angeles at the Democratic Party's National Convention, had finally materialized. JFK spoke at the huge Los Angeles Memorial Coliseum where 60,000 supporters had gathered to hear the young Democratic candidate espouse his views for the coming Sixties.

That starry night when Candidate Kennedy accepted his party's nomination, he had a clear vision of America's future and how the citizenry fit in:

> WE ARE NOT here to curse the darkness, but to light the candle that can guide us through that darkness to a safe and sane future . . .. Now man has taken into his

mortal hands the power to exterminate the entire spe-
cies some seven times over . . ..

Here at home the changing face of the future is
equally revolutionary . . . a technological revolution . . .
a peaceful revolution for civil rights . . . a medical revolution . . . a revolution of automation . . . we stand on
the edge of a New Frontier — the frontier of the Sixties — a frontier of unknown opportunities and perils, a
frontier of unfulfilled hopes and threats . . ..

The New Frontier of which I speak is not a set of
promises — it is a set of challenges. It sums up not what
I intend to offer the American people but what I intend
to ask of them. It appeals to their pride, not to their
pocketbook — it holds out the promise of more sacrifice instead of more security . . .. Beyond that Frontier are
the uncharted areas of science and space, unsolved problems
of peace and war, unconquered pockets of ignorance and
prejudice, unanswered question of poverty and surplus . . ..

I'm asking each of you to be pioneers of that New
Frontier. My call is to the young at heart . . .. For courage — not complacency — is our need today — leadership — not salesmanship . . .. Are we up to the task, are
we equal to the Challenge . . . or must we sacrifice our
future in order to enjoy the present? That is the question
of the New Frontier.

When JFK launched his June 10th "peace offering" at American
University, he had low expectations as to the impact it would have
on the Soviet Union; he knew his own State Department would
do its bureaucratic best to stymie his efforts to create peace. His
speech had been crafted in secret by his Presidential staff.

His gambit — to take the first step in creating a Limited Nuclear Test-Ban Treaty with USSR and England — was surprisingly well received in Russia. Soviet Premier Khrushchev immediately ordered JFK's translated speech shown on TV in every
major Russian city, buttressed by his own glowing endorsement.

On August 5th in Moscow, the day before the 18th anniversary of the Hiroshima bombing, a Limited Nuclear Test Ban Treaty between the three nations was signed. The U.S. Senate approved the Treaty September 24, 1963. Peace, which the world craved, was looming on the horizon, like a mirage turning into a road. October 7th in the White House Treaty Room, JFK signed the Limited Test Ban Treaty. October 11th, the Treaty went into effect; the following day JFK issued secret instructions to begin withdrawing 1,000 U.S. troops from Vietnam in December.

In early November, some of my beer-drinking buddies from UCLA's legendary men's "spirit" organization, Noble Order of KELPS, urged me to quit railroading and to become, along with them, white-collar workers selling Dictaphone recording machines to business people.

Dictaphone, a nationwide company, had been in the personal recording machine business for 45 years. Their rules for employees showed promise: wear a suit and tie, and even a colored dress shirt was acceptable, have drinks at lunch, and, best of all, pick your own hours because you have your own territory.

Getting a territory, which included a commission on all sales in your territory, was key. As the salesmen repeatedly sang in *The Music Man*, it's all about "the territory." After six and a half years of switching boxcars for the Santa Fe, first in San Berdoo (Bernardino) and now in L.A., I hung up my blue denim shirt, and put my railroad lantern into the trunk.

Hollywood was my territory, Davis Factor, chairman of Max Factor Cosmetics, and Technicolor VP and actor George Murphy were my prime targets for Dictaphone's new sleek P-7 personal recording machine.

Two weeks later, a former U.S. Marine, who had defected to the Russians in 1959 and who came back to America in 1962 hassle-free, supposedly murdered JFK in Dallas. Lee Harvey

Oswald was my age; we both served our time in the military. What motive would a 24 year old have to kill The President and, then, casually sit back in the cafeteria at the Book Depository and have a Coke?

Even more puzzling, why was President Kennedy even in such a hateful place as Dallas, Texas, a proud Confederate city that openly displayed on giant billboards and in full-page newspaper ads the scurrilous belief that the "Chief Justice of the U.S. Supreme Court is a traitor?" Kennedy being a Catholic from New England added more antipathy to Texas' historic Anglo-Saxon Protestant hatred of Northerners, especially Catholic Northerners.

The Sixties' New Frontier was over in four days: Friday assassination in plain view, Sunday morning televised murder inside the Dallas police station of suspected assassin Oswald — a self-proclaimed "patsy," followed on Monday by the President's solemn burial televised worldwide.

I went into shock and lamely sold Dictaphones in Hollywood. Then things went further south. Turns out Dictaphone's new P-7 didn't work.

When Dictaphone's National VP of Sales flew into town and personally informed the L.A. District that we were last in sales of Dictaphone's 45 sales districts, I stood up and asked why were we being forced to sell a machine that didn't work?

Dressed in his deep-blue double-breasted Brooks Brothers suit, silver tie, and black wingtips, his frosty white mane combed straight back looking like a smooth operator from New York City that he was, the VP of National Sales revealed, "Dictaphone had to meet the competition of IBM's new magnetic taping machines." New were magnetic tapes that could be taped over — distinct from Dictaphone's blue plastic Dicta-belt, which produced a permanently etched copy for only a nickel.

A sea change in business correspondence and record keeping had occurred, and Dictaphone responded by offering a machine that didn't work. "Besides" the VP added, "our Service Department will bail you salesmen out. Once you sell the machine, it's a Service Department problem."

As IBM shot past us in sales, we stopped selling our regular Dictaphone customers the new unworkable, heavily advertised P-7 personal recording machine. Instead, under-the-table, we sold them re-built P-6 recording machines, surreptitiously restored by *our* vaunted Service Department. The P-6s were clunky, dependable, and cheap. Being rich and famous, Davis Factor and George Murphy both insisted on owning the brand -new P-7. This was my first exposure to the non-unionized corporate world.

2

A POLITICAL REVOLUTION

As Marie's June 1964 graduation approached, so did our matrimony, planned to follow two days later. In April, we had rented a sunny, second-story apartment in Santa Monica where I had first lived after leaving San Berdoo and moving to L.A.

The day after we put down the rental deposit on our new home in Santa Monica, we received an official invitation from the Peace Corps to join a Community Development Training Program at Cornell University in upstate New York bound for rural Peru. Training would start in 60 days — seven days after Marie's June 11th graduation — five days after our June 13th marriage set for the romantic Pacific Palisades on Via de la Paz, overlooking the bodacious 25-mile-wide Santa Monica Bay.

Of course we accepted the Peace Corps' invitation.

Since the Peace Corps was paying for our flight to New York City, we switched our lowbrow honeymoon from Santa Monica's Beach Auto Hotel to the majestic St. Moritz Hotel whose 33 stories overlooked New York's gorgeous Central Park, urban America's greatest. The hotel, at 50 Central Park South, had in 1930 replaced the venerable New York Athletic Club with an Art-Deco masterpiece. The iconic St. Moritz Hotel, with its precedent-setting Café de la Paix sitting on the sidewalk facing the park, was NYC's most continental hotel. This epitome of elegance later morphed into the storied Ritz-Carlton.

It was an exhilarating return to my birthplace, and to that of my parents, their parents, and their parents' parents: 1st American born — March 1843 Astoria, New York — proudly named after Patrick Henry, the liberty-demanding revolutionary of 1775.

In this joyous, government-paid, return to the heart of Manhattan, I never spent so much money in my working-class life. But in four days, we'd be on a two-year expedition into the An-

des, time traveling back to the wretched days of Spanish Colonial serfdom. We imagined ourselves as heroic 20th century
volunteers from North America helping the downtrodden Andean serfs of South America obtain the necessary tools to rise
up and free themselves from oppression. We were stoked to be
starting an international adventure into the uncharted waters of
cross-cultural peacemaking. We were thrilled to be personally
rolling the dice on our game of life.

Cornell University was located upstate in Ithaca. The laid-back
18th century village lay alongside the southern end of Lake Ca-
yuga, a spectacular 40-mile-long Finger Lake, surrounded by a
robust forest of green, deep in the heart of the storied Catskill
Mountains.

The University was especially suited to train Peace Corps
Volunteers (PCVs). Cornell had a school for every specializa-
tion imaginable — offering a Bachelor's degree in hotel management, flower growing, sheep raising — you name it, they had
100 different degree specializations. Ezra Cornell's experimental
'land grant' school of 1865, "to teach all knowledge," had evolved
into a perfect place for teaching people how to raise their own
food.

Even more on target, since 1952 Cornell University had been
helping the rural Andean village of Vicos, Peru to enfranchise
its Indigenous population through enhanced potato production
and the purchasing of land from a neighboring *hacienda* (large
ranch).

Frank Mankiewicz, country director for the Peace Corps in
Peru, told our group of 102 trainees that we were going to "fo-
ment revolution in Latin America by aiding the poor." In his
speech, "Peace Corps — A Revolutionary Force," he explained
the crucial role Peace Corps Volunteers would play in President
Kennedy's new aid program for South America: Alliance for
Progress (*Alianza para el Progreso*):

OUR MISSION is essentially revolutionary. The ultimate
aim of community development is nothing less than a

16

complete change in the social and economic patterns of the countries to which we are accredited . . . .

Peace Corps workers will not contribute to the preservation of a system that cannot last and must not last. That's why Community Development (CD) is essentially a revolutionary process, consisting of helping these outsiders to get in.

Our job is to give them an awareness of where the tools are to enable them to assert their political power. When I talk about political power I am talking about the ability to be noticed and to be taken into account.

How do you go about giving tools that work for self-government? This is the mission of community development . . . nothing less than a political turnabout in the country to which we are assigned. We are talking about situations in which 3 percent of the people function effectively in a country and 97% do not. If that situation is to change, the non-participants must become participants, and the oppressed and forgotten become a functioning part of the country; this then is nothing less than a revolution, one accomplished by political means.

Volunteers must make immediate physical, visible, common cause with the people he or she is there to work with. That means live in their village or live in their slum area.

Talking about vacation, Mankiewicz made PCV protocol clear:

VOLUNTEERS ON LEAVE ought to live like a Volunteer not on leave — the only difference being that he or she is traveling. Identification is a crucial factor because, to an extent, a community development effort in Latin America is an international sit-in.

The task of the Volunteer is to call attention to this fragmented community . . . to function, in the best

Christian sense of the word, as a "witness" to the existence of the majority of the nation's citizens . . ..

Giving can become just another form of pushing the
problem under the rug. You are community organizers
dedicated to months of social investigation.

Community development requires endless atten-
dance at meetings that don't materialize. Community
action workers must get the people together . . . finally get them to assign themselves tasks while appearing
himself in a subordinate and advisory role . . ..

An integral part of community development is
demonstrating that things can be accomplished by people working together . . .. In that way, political participation, little by little, begins.

Organization, action, and technical assistance are all
required for community development: organizing and
demonstrating and finally helping with the actual work.

Political and social development of the country can
only come through the infusion of a kind of revolutionary spirit such as what the Peace Corps represents and
which more and more Latin American governments
now welcome.

This was true-blue post-WWII America — working at the
grassroots, leading the way to peace and prosperity for the whole
world. Peace Corps Volunteers were in the first wave, hitting
poverty's worst beachheads in Latin America, as well as in Asia,
Africa, and India. America to the rescue, peaceful revolutionary
change was coming. President Eisenhower's domineering style
of foreign affairs was over. Eugene Burdick's old school "ugly
Americans" were being replaced by "a new generation."

President Kennedy understood the mechanics behind the
Third World's quest for freedom and independence from its co-
lonial masters. He had patterned his Alliance for Progress after
FDR's New Deal, using public funds to promote social change.
Kennedy had convinced Congress to advance the Alliance bil-

lions of dollars in aid for Latin America to cover the costs their countries incurred instituting social reforms, like nationalization of foreign-owned businesses, Indigenous healthcare, agrarian reform, public education, infrastructure projects.

At the 1st Anniversary of the Alliance for Progress JFK reminded Latin America's foreign ministers of the consequences should those demands for reform be stifled: "Those who make peaceful revolution impossible will make violent revolution inevitable."

President John Kennedy speaking to Foreign Ministers of *Alianza para el Progreso*. White House, March 13, 1962 *White House Photo. JFK Library*

When the Cornell professors of rural anthropology told us that in helping the Andean people we could use cooperatives, I immediately questioned whether cooperatives were Communistic. My conservative Southern California suspicions were quickly allayed when Sunkist Oranges and Welch's Grape Juice were offered as examples of how agricultural marketing cooperatives helped the American economy create the world's wealthiest country.

I had been a part of that sun-kissed world of citrus. From age 11 to 16, every weekend, every holiday, every summer vacation, I sold Sunkist oranges at a small fruit stand in the orange groves 20 minutes southeast of our home in San Berdoo.

I worked for a fruit peddler, Armand Casper, a post-WWII immigrant from Switzerland. He picked me up early in his GMC truck, bought me a hearty breakfast of fresh orange juice, eggs, sausage, and pancakes at Pinky's Cafe at the Tri-Cities Airport at the southern end of Berdoo. In the 1930s, Evelyn "Pinky" Brier was a pioneering woman aviator. Her sister was the astrologer Jeanne Dixon; her brother was Ernie Pinckert, Berdoo's only All-American football player and college Hall of Fame inductee.

After that whopping breakfast, Mr. Casper dropped me off at our orange grove where I opened up the orange stand, and he went to the local packinghouse to re-supply. Except for the money, nothing was taken home at night. Everything was hidden amongst the orange trees disguised as a bunch of empty wooden field boxes. Two trees alongside the highway had been removed long ago giving us plenty of room to spread out our bags and boxes of oranges for curbside service. We had an eight-foot-tall wooden umbrella that stood above a short wooden sorting ramp, where a field box of oranges could be easily funneled into orange-colored mesh bags. Each wooden field box yielded four bags. Mr. Casper quadrupled the cost of each box of washed oranges he bought at the neighborhood Sunkist packinghouse.

An orange grower's harvest was washed, sorted, graded, and packaged at the Sunkist cooperative-owned packinghouse. Top grade oranges were wrapped in tissue paper and shipped to New York by rail, earning the highest price. Those oranges rejected by the process, usually for cosmetic reasons, were called "culls." That's what we sold from the small fruit stand, stuck in the hip pocket of an orange grove, a small port in a green sea of orange trees. The exotic fragrance of orange blossoms seduced our patrons.

All I had to do to make a sale was to cut an orange in half, and say to the traveler, "Try this." The juicy Valencias and the sweet Navels sold themselves. I wasn't as much a salesman as I was a curbside deliveryman.

Casper's orange stand was located alongside the westbound lanes of Highway 99 (now U.S. Interstate 10), five minutes west of the City of Redlands often referred to as the "Golden Buckle" of Southern California's legendary Citrus Belt that ran from Redlands to Ventura. The wealthy citrus grove owners of Redlands lived in gorgeous 19th century redwood mansions with Gothic spires, romantic stained-glass windows, and multiple fireplaces. Nestled securely into the eastern-most end of the Los Angeles Basin, at the entrance to the high desert, Redlands at one point had the highest number of millionaires per capita of any California city.

Besides my pay (started @ $4 a day and rose to $10 a day) and my tips (this was the road from Palm Springs to Beverly Hills), I also brought home a 15 lb. bag of juice oranges every weekend. By age 16 I was six feet tall, and wore a size 12D shoe. While I wasn't old enough to benefit from agricultural marketing coops, the curbside selling job on Highway 99 was a Godsend. I learned to communicate with all types and I earned enough to buy my first 'wheels.' At 16 I was, technically, free. Southern California car culture ruled. Von Dutch stripping, Angora dice, and four cement blocks in the trunk made us cool, low-riders.

I had spent thousands of hours on the side of Highway 99 waiting for customers, as diesel trucks, buses, and cars roared by on their way to L.A., 75 miles away. Thousands of hours standing on the curb, humming Ernie T. Ford's "Sixteen Tons," and thinking of John Steinbeck's Joad family crossing the broiling Mojave Desert. That story got me reading Steinbeck's *Cup of Gold*, his debut novel, *Pastures of Heaven*, his first collection of short stories, and *To a God Unknown*, his third book, a deep dive into the spiritual benefits of farming. Five and a half years of curbside learning.

3

BEING A PCV

Getting ready for Peru was a much more intense process. Nine weeks of 16 hours-a-day training at Cornell University was followed by three weeks of grueling Outward Bound training at Camp Radley in the jungles of Puerto Rico — rappelling down the face of Arecibo Dam, sleeping alone in the jungle, drown-proofing for 60 minutes with your hands tied behind your back — concluding with two weeks of rural community development fieldwork on the tiny neighboring Spanish-speaking Island of Vieques where we helped citizens pour cement for their rebar/cement-block constructed homes they were building with government provided materials. It was a place so beautiful, its beaches so picturesque that Hollywood made war movies there, and the U.S. Navy used it for bombing practice.

In early October we arrived in Lima, capital of modern Peru, a gray and gloomy city close to the Pacific Coast.

Psychological evaluators and FBI investigators had whittled our original training group of 102 trainees down to 69 sworn-in Volunteers. De-selection was a horrible, Kafkaesque process of weeding out the basket cases who had been selected to join training. Naturally, everyone wore their best plastic smile and tried not to reveal any personal secrets while taking the MMPI (Minnesota Multiphasic Personality Inventory). Usually, those Trainees found to be not truthful were de-selected.

Frank Mankiewicz, the Peru Country Director we knew from training, had been promoted to Peace Corps' Regional Director of Western Hemisphere programs. His replacement was Sam Guarnaccia, a burly former fullback from Middlebury College in Vermont, whose handshake was an unforgettable bone-crushing squeeze. Sam, son of a coal miner, greeted men and women with equal enthusiasm; he didn't discriminate. For twenty years he had been director of Middlebury College's highly regarded Summer Language Program.

The Peace Corps was filled with accomplished individuals, both staff and Volunteers. Peace was indeed the new wave. You could tell by the caliber of people who volunteered to serve and make America's grassroots effort a worldwide embrace.

Even so, everyone in the Peace Corps office was talking about Peter Sellers' new comedy "The Pink Panther" that had just opened at Cine El Pacifico in Lima's upscale neighborhood of Miraflores. The villain, David Niven, boasts that his nephew, played by Robert Wagner, "is considering joining the Peace Corps," but then warns him, "better be careful you don't give the family a good name." The New Frontier was box office hot. We couldn't have felt better about our upcoming adventure.

The Peace Corps sent Marie and me, and Mike and Sheila Heyn, the two married couples of our training group (Cornell, Rural Community Development, 1964-66) to the Mantaro Valley, over 10,000 feet, located in the Central Andes. Marie and the Heyns were Californians, and I passed for one, having lived there since the end of WWII. They were Northern Californians; we were Southern Californians separated by more than 400 miles; in Peru they were to be our closet American neighbors an hour's walk away.

The center of commerce for this highly productive agricultural region was the 400 year-old city of Huancayo, an urban center with over 100,000 residents. The people living in the surrounding communities and Huancayo were descendants of the Wari culture, which held power from 500 BC to 1100 AD. In 1250 they were forcibly merged into the Inca Empire; Spain then conquered the Incas in 1534.

Our 266-mile *Ferrocarril Central* (Central Railroad) journey from Lima was a laborious uphill trip until it reached the expansive, almost 40-mile-long Mantaro Valley. In 1964 it took our steam-engine-powered train ten hours to go from Lima to Huancayo, huffin' and puffin' the whole way. Incas used to travel the route on foot, and would strap their goods onto a llama, a camel descendant who refused to be ridden. The Industrial Revolution put that quaint mode of foot travel out of business with the arrival of the fire-breathing Iron Horse.

American "Robber Baron" Henry Meiggs, the legendary "Yankee Pizarro," had built the Ferrocarril Central railroad a hundred years earlier. His role in opening up pastoral Peru to the mechanized West reveals how Peru's consolidation of wealth by a few produced poverty for the many.

Peace Corps Volunteers (PCVs) were attempting to reverse that disparity.

Unfortunately many of Peru's economic and social problems had been centuries in the making. The do-nothing Spanish (1534–1826) were long gone thanks to Liberator Simon Bolivar's continental house cleaning of the early 19th century. But Spanish indolence was replaced by Western industrial indifference; and by a nasty homegrown *caudillo* (military) culture of embittered *mestizos* imbued with virulent racism (offspring of Spanish adventurers mating with Indigenous women).

After almost three centuries of being on the bottom of society — Spanish law had given the defeated Incas local control of the villages — the absence of Spain and its laws resulted in Indigenous people being moved to the bottom of the socio-economic ladder and being treated worse than slaves by the vengeful mestizos.

In 1851, Henry Meiggs left Baltimore on a ship with his family and a load of lumber and arrived in San Francisco Bay three months later, looking for gold along with the rest of the world.

Born in the heavily wooded Catskill Mountains of New York, Meiggs' forte was lumber. He soon established Mendocino Lumber Company 150 miles up the north coast by boat. They were the first to begin harvesting Mendocino's 2,000-year-old 20 foot-wide coastal redwoods (Sequoia sempervirens), mill-ing them in Mendocino, originally named Meiggsville, before shipping them by boat to the rapidly burgeoning city of San Francisco.

Ever the entrepreneur, Meiggs used his newly milled redwoods to enter San Francisco's wharf-building business; Meigg's Wharf of 1854 at the foot of Powell Street (now Fisherman's Wharf) originally reached 200 feet out into the Bay. Speculative real estate investments in North Beach that didn't bear fruit and Meiggs' illegal business practice of paying bills with worthless city of San Francisco warrants, finally put him on the run.

In 1855 having $400,000 worth of angry creditors hot on his heels, Meiggs grabbed all of Mendocino Lumber Company's cash ($8,000), chartered a ship and captain, and fled with his family south to Valparaíso, Chile's port, 6,000 miles away as the albatross flies.

Within three years, "Don Enrique" Meiggs emerged as a successful railroad builder constructing Chile's first train line from the Andean foothills of Santiago to Valparaíso. By the mid-1860s he realized that Chinese immigrant workers — who were no longer needed to build America's now completed transcontinental railroad — could easily be re-routed by W.R. Grace's steamship lines from the Bay Area south to Calláo, Peru's port 4,500 miles away.

Since Inca descendants had proven unsuitable for slave labor, Meiggs, armed with a steady supply of Chinese laborers, now felt emboldened enough to conquer the Andes, the world's largest and longest mountain range. He seemed to have found his calling and successfully built railroads throughout the precipitous, craggy Andes — 1,200 miles overall, 700 miles in Peru alone. His trademark — redwood ties from California. Using the Iron Horse to assist in the extraction of Peru's many minerals made Henry Meiggs rich and powerful. The Yankee Pizarro died in Lima in 1877, a consort of Andean Presidents, employer of thousands. Some even characterized the flamboyant builder Don Enrique as, "*el dictador del Peru*."

Don Enrique Meiggs' Iron Horse steams past Mt. Ticlio. Image from Eloy Barona, Sicaya

To conquer the enormous Central Andes of Peru, and the sheer 16,499-foot mountain that now bears his name, Meiggs' Ferrocarril Central inserted six switchbacks into the ascent, pushing and pulling the five-car train up the steep mountainside. Not an efficient route, but one that allowed the Iron Horse to rise from sea level to Mt. Ticlio's breathless 15,807-foot-high mountain pass, the second highest rail line in the world.

From there they pierced through the pinnacle of the Andes, Mt. Meiggs, down the eastern side to Galera, the world's highest rail station at 15,681 feet, and then cautiously passed through Galera's spooky 3,847-foot-long tunnel, an engineering marvel constructed at 15,692 feet!

Slowly the tracks descend to La Oroya at 12,195 feet where the train line either turns south toward Huancayo or trudges north to the foreboding Cerro de Pasco gold, silver, zinc, and copper mines at 14,232 feet. Discovered in 1635 by diligent Jesuits, it was the largest silver mine in the world and is still functioning. (According to Blacksmith Institute, C de P is the world's most polluted mine; its 50,000 workers possess the highest lead levels on Earth.)

The smelter to extract mineral substances was in La Oroya, where clouds of toxic sulfuric acid spewed from its 543-foot-tall smokestack (making La Oroya, in 2007, the "most polluted place of Earth"). Against the barren brown and black mountain scape, the enormous La Oroya smokestack looked like a gigantic syringe stuck deep into the earth, smoking in pain. Indigenous people believe the smoke came from the incineration of their relatives.

The Huancayo Station at 10,200 feet was the last stop of Meiggs' spectacular Central Andean railway journey of 63 tunnels (totaling 21,000 feet), 58 bridges, and 21 switchbacks, and an estimated 10,000 dead laborers. (Today's Ferrocarrill Central: Calláo-Lima-Huancayo-Huancavelica operates once a month.)

Fourteen miles northeast of Huancayo, snow-covered *Mt. Huaytapallana* (quiver of wild flowers) reigns over the Central Andes reaching an altitude of 18,232 feet.

Sicaya, where Marie and I had been assigned, was a progressive community of 5,000 *campesinos* (farmers), two of whom owned cars . . . a '55 Ford Fairlane and a late '40s Dodge sedan. Sicaya was 35 minutes from Huancayo on the *margen derecha* ("right" west side) of the Mantaro River. Sicaya's pre-Colonial origins (the Sika culture) date back to the Wari culture 1000 CE, perhaps even earlier.

Manzanares, where the Heyns were stationed, is also a *margen derecha* community, an hour walk across the *pampa* from Sicaya. We were now next-door neighbors, although we mainly saw each other in Huancayo, the only place in the valley with electricity and hot water.

Regardless of whether there was a train to Huancayo or not, every Sunday while we were there 30,000 Quechua-speaking Native Americans from the upper altitudes descended upon Huancayo to sell their handmade wares in what was called the "Silent" Sunday Fair. Indigenous people felt that . . . "hawking" their goods was undignified, something only a mestizo would do. This weekly commercial gathering inundated the entire city of Huancayo, which had only two public toilets.

It was the caudillo way of pretending the Indigenous people did not exist. Each Sunday the Indigenous people used one dirt street as their bathroom. For decades, I thought the Indigenous people were backward for pooping in the street, until I finally realized it was the mestizos who held the purse-strings of Huancayo. It was just one more payback for all those years they spent at the bottom of the Spanish Empire.

Every Sunday the PCVs of the Mantaro Valley also flocked to Huancayo's Silent Fair for its food and its art. Inca weavers had produced the world's most finely woven fabrics, and their modern descendants still upheld ancient traditions of high-quality handspun alpaca wool. In stall after stall women sold blankets, sweaters, skirts, scarves, caps, and mittens in vivid red, pink and purple colors, all decorated with symbols of their community. There were also large gourds that depicted historical scenes carved by a hot charcoal point, and small gourds that carried Incan designs and were used as baby rattles. Silversmiths sold spoons, tiny llama bells, silver filigree necklaces, rings, and earrings. *Curandaras* (healers) sold health and happiness.

Over 400 years after their defeat, Huancayo's "Silent" Sunday Fair revealed the Inca culture was still doing a brisk and steady business.

The main watering hole for the PCVs was the Olímpico Restaurante with its cosmopolitan seating practices. Indigenous and Mestizo Peruvians sat at the same shared public tables, an Andean rarity where Indigenous people were regularly, politically and economically, disrespected.

Besides shopping in the Silent Fair, there was a quick stop at the Peace Corps office to pick up mail, then a possible movie theater escape, ending with Huancayo's open-air bathhouse for our weekly hot water shower. At this altitude it is so cold and dry you never perspire; you showered for warmth . . . a weekly ritual.

Sitting at the community table of the Olímpico Restaurante, eating *papa a la huancaina* (boiled potatoes with Huancayo-style sauce), *lomo saltado* (seasoned beef strips), and slurping spicy *sopa criolla* (soup) was our only opportunity to mix with one another. Here, in English, we could share our lives, our progress and problems working the muddy grassroots of the Mantaro Valley.

The biggest news, and a sad commentary on where we lived, was that John of the British Volunteer Services, who drove around the Mantaro Valley in a Range Rover — vehicles were a luxury PCVs did not have — had been in a serious accident driving on the *margen izquierda* ("left" east side) of the Mantaro River. People thought he was dead so they stole his boots right off his feet, a la *The Treasure of the Sierra Madre*.

It was a wake-up call to all of us that we were living in a "Make-No-Mistake" environment. Poverty produces a lean and mean world.

If you went to a hospital in Peru you were on your own . . . you even had to bring your own food. Volunteers were somewhat lucky, Peace Corps had a doctor in Lima, which meant a perilous six-hour journey roaring down the mountains in a shared five-passenger taxi, on a one-lane no-guardrail highway to Lima, dodging trucks and rocks, buses and burros.

Eventually John was flown to London after being airlifted out of Jauja, an 11,200-foot-high city at the northwestern end of the Mantaro Valley that had a small airport.

Juaja is where the Incas last fought, and lost, to the Spanish in 1534. As a consequence, ancient Juaja, where an Inca road veers into the Amazon basin, and only 28 miles from Huancayo, became New Spain's first capital. But Jauja proved to be too far from the Port of Calláo where all the action was. In 1535 fog-shrouded Lima, only 11 miles from the coast, became the City of Kings, capital of Spain's new Vice Royalty.

The amount of gold taken from the Inca Empire put Spain at the top of the world's monarchies. Many of Spain's best families re-located to the New World. There was just so much gold, and there was just so much more if you lived there. In training we were told, "Forty families ruled Peru." Cornell professors never gave us their names.

Our large, 15 feet by 20 feet, upstairs, white-washed adobe-walled room was in the center of town and faced Sicaya's plaza. We were surrounded by: Santo Domingo Church, *el consejo del junta comunal* (community council), Guardia Civil (police station and jail), and the Posta Sanitaria, a small health station.

There Marie used her 20th century knowledge and experience to work in the areas of health and wellness, administration of vaccinations, and family nutrition.

Sweet William and Marie in front of the Turista Hotel de Huancayo on their 1st Wedding anniversary June 13, 1965

As a Community Development Volunteer I assisted various groups in the community whose goals were to establish projects in support of improving the lives of the citizens.

For one, I began to push the newly announced rural electric co-op for the Mantaro River valley.

Although I didn't know it at the time, the proposed cooperative was part of President Kennedy's overall economic development plan to meet the Third World's rising expectations. November 1962 the President forged a partnership with the National Rural Electrical Cooperative Association (NRECA) and their almost 300 domestic cooperatives to form an International component to work exclusively with Kennedy's newly created Agency of International Development (AID). Together, they would disseminate America's knowledge and experience in electrifying rural life to the Third World. Mantaro River valley was the third rural electric cooperative proposed for Latin America. In a way, it was a no-brainer. Western civilization needed electricity to truly operate — to show its movies, to power its machines, to light its nights.

Each community in the 37-mile-long Mantaro Valley that wanted electricity had to sign up at least one-hundred households: a socio (membership) that cost S/70 soles (US $9). The average annual Andean individual income was between $400 and $800.

Town folk did not need convincing. Sicaya was a respected and progressive community and had ample acreage, private and *comunal* (community owned), where they grew barley, maize, quinoa, potatoes, and other vegetables.

At 6 a.m. each day Angel Navarro, Sicaya's fiscal (treasuer), the largest man in town, and I went door-to-door to catch farmers before they left home to work their fields and graze their animals.

After our early morning search for *socios* (members), Angel would cap off our frigid work by ordering us a couple of *copitas de aguardiente* (firewater) at the local *tienda* (small store with a dirt floor).

These simple beginnings often led to hours-long drinking bouts. Although I saw myself as a serious college drinker, *los Sicaínos* (those living in Sicaya) showed me that I was not in the same league as the everyday Andean beer drinker. I tried many times to keep up with them, but their rules of drinking etiquette did me in and I stopped drinking beer.

In the rugged, slow-moving Andes, victories were celebrated as often as possible. Getting electricity would be a major accomplishment, an effort linked together by a lot of little victories and a lot more celebratory drinking. With much fanfare, and more drinking, *La Cooperativa Comunal del Centro #127*, Mantaro

Valley's rural electric co-op — Peru's first — was incorporated in Huancayo on the 1st Anniversary of President Kennedy's assassination . . . 11/22/1964.

4

SENATOR KENNEDY OF NEW YORK

During that same time period, President Kennedy's brother, Robert Kennedy, the former U.S. Attorney General, anguished over the unbelievable losses of his brother and of their shared vision of a New Frontier.

Even more painful to him was the possibility that his Department of Justice's war against organized crime had somehow contributed to his brother's murder. He had deported New Orleans mob boss Carlos Marcello, publicly battled Jimmy Hoffa, and it was no secret that Jack Ruby and his Dallas strip club were mob connected, as were the former gambling casinos of Havana.

Amidst this grief — all playing out in public view — Robert Kennedy had to decide on whether to re-enter the political arena. President Johnson did not want him on the 1964 Presidential ticket so RFK ran for the U.S. Senate seat in New York, his first candidacy for elective public office. It was an excruciating process for the former behind-the-scenes manager of his brother's successful campaigns. RFK was now dependent upon the public to have a political life.

A shy man of less than average build, RFK, nonetheless, jumped into the fray, countered charges of being a Bostonian carpetbagger, and emerged victoriously. The public wanted him to stay on the political stage, and who could be more American than the diverse population of the City of New York? People were not through with the Kennedys. RFK had long served his brother's agenda; now, as a U.S. Senator, he had to find out what he could bring to the table.

Once assuming the Presidency, Johnson immediately began rolling back President Kennedy's peacemaking initiatives. The day after JFK was buried, LBJ countermanded JFK's October 11, 1963 National Security Action Memorandum (NSAM) #263, "to begin withdrawing 1,000 U.S. troops from South Vietnam beginning December 1963, all troops by December 1965."

Instead, on November 26th, LBJ assembled Secretaries Robert McNamara (Defense), and Dean Rusk (State), and Director John McCone (CIA) and Ambassador Henry Cabot Lodge, jr. (S. Vietnam) to witness his issuance of NSAM #273 that gave a green light to supporting South Vietnam in its civil war with the North.

Infamously, LBJ made it clear "I'm not going to lose Vietnam. I'm not going to be the President who saw Southeast Asia go the way China went."

His NSAM #273 also allowed "covert activities" that eventually led to the Gulf of Tonkin and the U.S.S Maddox episode and to Congress granting LBJ "War Powers" three months before a Presidential election!

After his November 1964 re-election as a "candidate of peace," versus kooky Arizona Senator Barry Goldwater, LBJ aggressively began to carve out his own diplomatic legacy. In March of 1965, he issued NSAM #288 that transformed America's advisory role in Vietnam into our own war against the dirty Commies, "wherever they may be hiding in Southeast Asia."

His April 28, 1965 invasion of the Dominican Republic with U.S. Marines in an attempt to forestall a "communist dictatorship" reverberated throughout South America all the way up to our tiny Andean village. Citizens woke us up by throwing rocks at our door and yelling in Spanish-accented English, "Yankee Go Home." You couldn't blame them. The invasion was a clear rebuke of JFK's Latin American strategy of financing peaceful homegrown revolutions with Alliance for Progress funds.

Most of early 1965, RFK dealt with family issues, helping to establish the JFK Library, and becoming the first to climb Canada's newly named Mt. Kennedy.

In Congress he supported gun control and immigration reform; on June 23rd he gave his first Senate speech, a comprehensive argument devoted to the dangers of nuclear proliferation; and in August he and his younger brother, U.S. Senator Edward "Ted" Kennedy of Massachusetts, attended the White House signing of the Voting Rights Bill into law. RFK was carrying on Jack's work but doing it his way. Equally as witty, RFK had a zeal his brother, the President, had not brandished.

In preparing to take his first overseas visit as a U.S. Senator, a trip to Latin America in late 1965, RFK asked Frank Mankiewicz, one of the government officials attending an August inter-agency briefing, what he thought of the State Department's recommended itinerary of business and government leaders.

Mankiewicz remarked, "The trip wouldn't be worth taking." In the next breath, the garrulous "Mank" added, "I'd explore the plight of the poor. In Peru, I would go to Comas, a huge *barriada* (shanty town) on the outskirts of Lima."

The Senator took the bait. Peru would be his first stop.

5

HIGH IN THE ANDES

Our Peace Corps assignment was in the Mantaro Valley, a productive 37-mile-long, 6-mile-wide farming area. A valley this wide was rare in the sheer-sided Andean mountains, where "falling out of your *chakra* (field)" was a common cause of death . . . a fact I disbelieved in training.

D.J. Boyd, a co-op PCV (L.A. State 1964-66) was stationed in the nearby mining community of Huancavelica, 12,073 feet in altitude, but he worked at mines that were located at over 14,000-feet high organizing consumer co-ops. He and I had scheduled an appointment in faraway Lima to meet with Peruvian government officials about using the U.S. Food for Peace program in our respective communities.

Food for Peace, the brainchild of U.S. Senator George McGovern of South Dakota, utilized excess farm products: flour, butter, corn meal, peanut butter, powdered milk as part of America's foreign aid program. In Peru, Food for Peace was primarily used as bait to get impoverished Andean children of the Indigenous Quechua-speaking population to go to school for some food and to end up learning to speak Spanish.

The timing of our meeting in Lima would enable us attend the famous Plaza de Acho bullfights. Its bullfighting ring was the oldest in South America, and had hosted *corridas del toros* (bullfights) since 1766 — a traditional, centuries-old battle between man and beast.

The annual *Señor de los Milagros Feria* (Lord of Miracles [Christ] Festival) was held for six consecutive weekends of bullfighting that started each October. As all *aficionados* (fans/followers) knew, the best bulls, the locally bred bulls, were saved for November.

We did not know at the time it would be the Bicentennial of Western Hemisphere Bullfighting. But we did know that it would feature the daring young Spanish *matador* Manuel Benítez, known worldwide as El Cordobés — a person from Cordoba, who as an orphan rose to become the world's highest paid *toreador*.

As planned, we went to Plaza del Acho, as did secretaries who worked in the Peace Corps' main office. Nina Portero, office manager, sat in front of us.

At the beginning of the contest, the *matador*, with a *banderilla* in each hand held high above his head, ran forward and leaped between the charging bull's horns, deftly sticking his banderillas in the bull's thick neck muscle in the hour-long battle to lower the bull's huge head enough for the final *coup d'grace*.

We got rip-roaring drunk drinking wine from a *bodega* bag, and enamored by the *coraje* (courage) of the toreadors, we bought souvenir banderillas — thin, thirty-inch-long by one-inch-wide wooden poles wrapped in red crepe paper, and anchored by a sharp, one-inch steel barb.

The straining *picador*, sitting atop his padded horse, looked like an image from Cervantes' *Don Quixote*. He cradled a long smooth pole in his arms. On the end was a two by four-inch surgically smooth metal *pica* (point) used for protection against the bull's charge and for jabbing the bull's massive neck muscle. The picador was no one's favorite.

Despite El Cordobés being thrown twice, his acrobatic footwork and swift sword work enabled him to defy death and win "Two Ears." A wild and courageous performance!

It was dark when we were leaving Plaza del Acho and the streets were jammed with traffic. On foot, we were armed with our colorful banderillas and were so *borracho* (drunk) we started mimicking El Cordobés in open traffic.

Like in Cuba, Peru's taxi fleet was primarily composed of early 20th century American automobiles. Lima had a wonderful collection of 1920s and 1930s Model T-Fords, old beyond belief.

Most of their car horns didn't work so drivers used banging on the outside of their car door with their opened palm instead.

Fearlessly, D.J. and I took turns charging on-coming traffic, banderillas held high, and as we reached forward and touched the top of the radiator cap with the banderillas, we twisted away, injury free, like a *macho* matador. We were disciples of the quick-footed El Cordobés.

As it turned out, our "official" business trip from the hinterlands unexpectedly coincided with Senator Kennedy's November 10th arrival in Lima, an event the State Department had purposely not publicized. LBJ worried that RFK would stir up trouble. Somehow the people of Peru had gotten the news and Peruvians of all ages and incomes greeted the Senator and his wife, Ethel, excitedly.

Immediately upon his arrival, the Senator began asking Embassy officials for a guide to visit barriadas. No one knew where they were located, so they called the Peace Corps office and Peace Corps/Lima Associate Representative James Lowry became the Senator's guide.

Peace Corps/Peru headquarters on *Avenida Wilson 1454* bristled with excitement, "The Senator wants to see what PCVs are doing."

The Senator's first stop was lunch at the Palacio de Gobierno with recently elected President Fernando Belaúnde-Terry whose citizen-friendly style of government was patterned after John Kennedy's New Frontier.

RFK's and Ethel's next stop was a park dedication ceremony in the *Apolo* section of La Victoria, a low-income neighborhood of Lima. A 12-foot iron silhouette statue of JFK was going to be installed and blessed. The statue's inscription from his Inaugural Address read (in Spanish): "Ask Not What Your Country Can Do For You; Ask What You Can Do For Your Country."

Thousands surrounded the new urban park named after JFK. Peruvians, having spotted the Embassy officials' arrival, quickly descended upon Lowry and his celebrated visitors.

A military brass band started playing and, as everywhere, local dignitaries and the public enthusiastically embraced, or you could say, swamped them. In response, Senator and Mrs. Kennedy smiled radiantly and, like all good Catholics, proudly boasted of their nine children.

Kennedy had his "Youth Speech" message down. He was anxious to engage the youth of Peru and of all the South American countries he planned to visit. At the *Instituto Peruano-NorteAmericano* he received an hour and a half harangue of angry engagement. Expecting Kennedy to back LBJ's April attack on the Dominican Republic, the leftist student leaders were caught off guard by RFK's suggestion that they, the young activists, go it alone, "Stop blaming the U.S. and make your own future."

In the evening, RFK and some of his traveling companions met privately with a group of Lima artists and intellectuals at the home of Peruvian abstract painter Fernando de Szyszlo. Drinking Pisco Sours, modern Peru's favorite beverage, they listened to their hosts complain of LBJ shutting off AID funds until Peru had executed a new contract with International Petroleum Company (IPC), a Standard Oil subsidiary.

It was the same message President Belaúnde gave him at lunch, but Peru's President couldn't make his complaints public. He had even made "Resolution of the IPC controversy in 90 days" a 1963 Campaign promise, to no avail. It was a crass attempt, they all argued, to force the Peruvian government to resolve its long-standing contractual dispute with IPC in the company's favor in exchange for the release of Alliance for Progress funds.

"Aid should not be withheld to force special advantage for U.S. businesses," grumbled the newly elected U.S. Senator of New York.

Many guests claimed Americans were handmaidens to the Rockefellers. "We Kennedys eat Rockefellers for breakfast," was RFK's glib response.

The next morning, Nov. 11th, RFK, his associates, Peace Corps officials, and members of the press flew to Cusco, capital of the ancient Inca Empire, 11,200 feet high in the towering Andes. Ancient Cusco, *ombligo* (navel) of the vast Inca Empire, was a mysterious city comprised of mammoth, precisely cut, smooth stone buildings, walls, roads, and fortresses — all built without any mortar, power saws, or hydraulic lifts. Some stones weighed 100 tons!

The Senator was intrigued by the scale and sophistication of the Sacsayhuaman stone fortress, strategically located at the northern entrance to Cusco at 12,142 feet, the highest point in the Sacred Valley of Cusco.

According to *El Sol's* November 12th edition, RFK, while standing at the foot of the Christ the Redeemer statue, admired the panorama of Cusco and asked, "What were they (Incas) like? What did they eat? How did they move these massive boulders?"

Once he and his party left Sacsayhuaman, the few local people who owned vehicles, joined the impromptu parade for *el hermano de JFK*. Happily and noisily they traversed the sparse treeless *altiplano*, ringing cowbells, some pounding on the sides of their car doors in excitement, others honking their horns, which many *serranos* (Andean people) considered an extravagance. Even so, it was JFK's brother and they were letting loose. Andean life was no walk in the park for the Indigenous people. Every step was steeped in grinding poverty and gross discrimination. Here, though, was a hero to champion.

On the Pan-American Highway, west of Cusco, the Senator and his growing entourage began visiting villages, pausing in Chacán for *tragos y chicha* (shots of *aguardiente* and glasses of Inca-style corn beer), and eventually stopping in Compone, population 1,055, (221 families).

"He arrived at the head of this long caravan of 26 vehicles," recalled PCV Karen Marcus, one of three PCVs from our Cornell group assigned to the pre-Colonial village of Compone. It was here that RFK would see rural-based Peace Corps Volunteers at work.

Harriet "Skeeter"Tower, Marilyn Keyes, and Karen (Cornell Rural CD 1964-66) were originally assigned to a new government reforestation project for the Cusco area to provide residents with critically needed firewood, construction lumber, and to prevent soil erosion. Peruvian officials described their eucalyptus reforestation project as *mit'a* (donating work to a community project and shared ownership of the resulting end product). Campesinos who planted saplings in the communal plot received Food for Peace surpluses; these were people who made $400 a year, basic dollar-a-day existence!

All the physical elements had come together: December 1963 Compone village leaders approved the reforestation program, special fast-growing saplings were delivered in the summer, PCVs arrived in the fall of 1964. But, as the district-wide forestation program was being implemented at the village level, complaints came forth, slowing the planting effort, and in some villages paralyzing the planting of eucalyptus saplings on communal land.

As in most new projects that cross cultural boundaries, there were unexpected problems at the community level. Which communal lands to use for a eucalyptus plantation resulted in longer distances for some people to take their animals to graze: the poorest depended most on communal lands and were impacted the most severely. Women didn't always have a vote in village assemblies and would, in revolt, graze their animals in the newly planted eucalyptus plots.

To make things almost impossible, Peru's Forestry Division would receive the first 30% of the revenue generated from these communal reforestation plots. Not surprisingly, communities disengaged at various levels of involvement in the government's new eucalyptus reforestation program for critically needed wood.

Fortunately for the three PCVs, the village of Compone had a reputation as an up-and-coming community. They had recently won a land dispute with the neighboring hacienda Sullupiciji, adding valuable land to its communal properties. Leaders saw the arrival of these *Hijas de JFK* (daughters of JFK) as a sign of their community's progressiveness and formed a tight partnership with the Volunteers. Skeeter summed up their 20 month assignment, "The key to our time in Compone was that we worked hand-in-glove with the community leaders: Señor Huaman, *junta comunal* chairman, Guido Ortiz, school director, and local veterinarian Julio Sumar." Director Ortiz, after finishing his college education, had returned to Compone to energize its educational resources so others might follow his example. Guido was a dynamo and successfully channeled the three PCVs into his effort to build out Compone's educational offerings. The three women didn't need any encouragement.

Frank Mankiewicz had told us in our training at Cornell that social change was the name of the game and it wouldn't be easy to play. He emphasized that the road to cross-cultural engagements would be challenging on many levels: psychological, cultural, racial, historical, economical, socio-political. Crossing over into new cultures and ignoring racial and gender stereotypes would produce unexpected twists and turns. Especially so for PCVs traveling down "Community Development's revolutionary road to social and economic betterment for the poor." So it was in Peru, Peace Corps' largest Western Hemisphere program, fielding over 2,600 PCVs between 1962 and 1968.

Many Volunteer assignments had the unpredictable element of what the local counterpart felt about this new arrival, *un gringo de Cuerpo de Paz* (Peace Corps) who doesn't need money but who purposely lives in poverty-stricken communities. Some cynics wondered whether these were budding young American capitalists sent to Third World countries to practice their craft on unsuspecting Indigenous people. Why else would these young wealthy North Americans seek out the poor? These Hijos de JFK (children of JFK) were confounding; they didn't act like "Ugly Americans," nor did they look like them.

The Peace Corps needed Volunteers for their Community Development programs who were innovators, go-getters, smart, brave, emotionally flexible people willing to work at the grassroots of a foreign society to help the poor rise up. It was tough, tedious work pursuing social change in a second language, especially if it's their second language, too.

Crossing cultural lines in a positive manner is an essential talent in the world of peacemaking where you need to identify allies everywhere in order for peace to prevail. Peace Corps Volunteers — trained Change Agents living amongst the masses — were key to JFK's vision of a "peaceful revolution" to creatively engage the Third World's rapidly rising expectations. Skeeter, Marilyn, and Karen, having been trained in the Mankiewicz model, exemplified this ethos by turning the failure of their initial reforestation project into many other successful endeavors in their community.

PCV Karen Marcus and Senator Robert Kennedy in Compone

Before PCVs arrived in Compone some residents had attempted whitewashing their exterior adobe walls with Food for Peace's powdered milk. Twenty months later when the PCVs left, Compone was no longer one of Peru's infamous dispossessed *las comunidadas olvidadas* (forgotten communities). No longer were they unknown. Throughout the Anta district, Compone now had a reputation for holding the education of their young as a core community belief.

Karen began working with young children, using a cup of morning cocoa to create a pre-school. Marilyn, fluent in Spanish, began teaching the Quechua-speaking women food preparation and elementary Spanish. Skeeter led the efforts to repair the school building. Together, these three recent college graduates and Guido became an educational force. To many neighboring villages, Compone had become an example of how investing communal wealth in education paid off.

The PCVs helped *Cooperacíon Popular* — President Belaúnde's new community action agency patterned after the U.S. Peace Corps — repair Compone's adobe school building. When the junta *comunal* declared a faena to build a second story addition to the school, a new library room, *las tres gringas* kicked off their boots and rolled up their pant legs. Making adobe with their bare feet, helping to build a staircase up to the new library room, and finally installing a new roof, culminated many months of working on smaller projects that financially supported the overall school construction efforts.

When the three Hijas de JFK departed Compone, the community had classrooms with desks, a pre-school 'cocoa' Head-Start program, a new library room with books and magazines, 4-H style chicken-raising/egg-producing clubs serving more than 100 families, an ad hoc seed and fertilizer buying cooperative, a gigantic hillside garden of cypress and eucalyptus tree saplings, and a nascent feeling amongst local women, after watching these three young *gringas* getting things done, that the world held unknown opportunities for them, too.

Probably the most "revolutionary development" to occur in Compone had to do with the building of the upstairs library room. In the treeless altiplano wood was always an expensive commodity. Unfortunately the wood they received from the forestry division to build the tresses for the new library roof was so green the men couldn't pound in a nail. As Mank told us in training, when things get tough the tough innovate. Nails could be hammered in, Guido discovered, by greasing them with Food for Peace butter!

Robert Kennedy's arrival in Compone coincided with the completion of the new Library Room. Residents felt enormous pride that their village had been selected by President Kennedy's brother to visit. The tiny village was filled with hundreds of people. Bands were playing; harps were thumping, drums were beating, everyone was dressed in their Sunday best. An advocate of early childhood education, Senator Kennedy thoroughly enjoyed celebrating Compone's educational achievements. Standing at the top of the new staircase leading to the new Library Room, he congratulated the community leaders for their foresight in investing in their youth. He went into each classroom and awarded a new silver Kennedy half-dollar to the best student of each class.

Later, Skeeter recalled, "RFK gave PT 109 tie clasps to many men of the community." Marilyn chimed in, "Yeah, they became great money clips. Men of Compone proudly bragged, "*El hermano de JFK me dío este regalo personalmente* (the brother of JFK personally gave me this gift). "

Karen remembered, "After leaving the school site Senator Kennedy came to our house and ate some brownies and looked at our family albums. I was surprised by his height, he was just a little taller than I," remarked the 5'8" brunette. "He was blonder than I imagined, and he had the bluest eyes I've ever seen. How could we not accept his invitation to dinner at Cusco's ritzy Turista Hotel?"

Marilyn remembered when they left, Senator Kennedy took some brownies with him, "*manna*," he pleaded.

On the drive back to Cusco, RFK shared his brownies with Richard Goodwin, a JFK speechwriter and architect of the Alliance for Progress, who RFK had invited as a guest on his South

American expedition. Importantly, Goodwin was to act as a forensic expert on the health of his brother's revolutionary *Alianza para el Progreso*.

Goodwin, who had a profound knowledge of Latin America, asked RFK, as he licked the chocolate off his fingertips, "What did the Senator think of the IPC controversy cutting off AID funds to Peru, a functioning democracy?"

Karen recalled RFK's pained response, "Withholding funds is injurious. President Belaúnde has good programs that should be supported. Without promised U.S. assistance, his reform plans are frustrated; Cooperacíon Popular is cutting back. Withholding funds totally subverts the reform agenda of the Alliance for Progress."

So stinging was his rebuke that Karen wrote it down and mailed it home to Seattle — "News from the Front!"

At the Turista Hotel, a government-operated chain of tourist-grade hotels, a group of university students was waiting. RFK told them what he said at the Cusco airport that morning when a throng of 2,000 Cusqueños exuberantly broke down the airport's chain-link fence to greet him *personalmente*.

"In these small villages," RFK intoned, "resides the future of Latin America. Listen," he told the students sternly, "if you don't like U.S. actions, do something about them."

During dinner Senator Kennedy, Richard Goodwin, and members of his entourage continued discussing the IPC controversy. Kennedy told them that after his inter-agency briefing last August, McGeorge Bundy, Presidential Advisor to both LBJ and JFK, gave him the lowdown, "Eisenhower's former Asst. Secretary of State for Latin America, Thomas Mann, was back in control. Any public criticism by you of these policies would delay improvement for at least an additional three months."

Mann's Doctrine allowed the U.S. to support dictators so long as they supported U.S. business interests. But his Doctrine would never permit financially supporting a Socialist/Communist country regardless of whose products they bought or how many people voted for them. Alianza para el Progreso was dead.

Its instruments of peaceful change were compromised by LBJ's corporate favoritism.

The male members of the dinner party in Cusco agreed that they had to make the issue public, but without RFK blowing the whistle. Who could take the heat, perhaps JFK's *hijos*?

The three female PCVs were too busy eating to join in the plotting. They were impressed by how knowledgeable all these men were. How curious RFK was, "Did the Indigenous people know about the United States?" How funny he was. When he was asked by a reporter: "To what do you attribute Republican John Lindsay's election as Mayor of New York?" RFK responded, in a mock professorial tone, "To the fact that he got the most votes."

6

¿QUE PASA AQUI?

In Lima, U.S. Embassy officials were planning Senator Kennedy's Nov. 12th visit to Comas, the infamous barriada that Mankiewicz had recommended visiting. Here Senator Kennedy would meet Peace Corps Volunteers who had been working in urban Peru.

Steve Russo, a 21 year-old ironworker from Queens, New York, the youngest member of our group (Cornell Rural CD 1964–66), had been selected to be the English-to-Spanish translator for the press bus.

From the moment our group arrived in October 1964, Russo dove into Spanish and learned more colloquial expressions than any Andean squatter ever did — keep in mind these Quechua speakers, like Steve, spoke Spanish as a second language. Russo took great pride in linguistically becoming a "local" where Peruvians thought of him as "one of us."

As Embassy officials scoured the maps to decide the best route to Comas, Russo interrupted their discussions by telling them their maps were out of date. A makeshift bridge, crossing a deep crevice, no longer existed. Eventually, after physically showing them the impassibility of their route, Russo laid out the official route to Comas for the Senator's caravan.

Short and muscular, gregarious and blunt, locals called Steve "a stick of dynamite." They were correct. He had a dynamic impact on everything he worked on in Peru. He and PCV roommate Leroy Lange (LA State Co-ops 1964-66), an architect from Minnesota, were actively engaged in building the huge *Parque de las leyendas* (Park of Legends) that featured the Three Worlds of Peru: Coastal, Andean, and Amazonian. Today, it is named Lima's Zoological Park.

Every January to March — Peru's summer — Russo and Lange helped John Donohue, also of our Cornell group, run Peru's Department of Education's wildly popular beachfront *Campo Alegre* (Happy).

They camped out at Ventanilla Beach, cooking outdoors with Army-donated kerosene, and living under huts made of estera (straw mats). Their weekly program of swimming, volleyball, and soccer for 125 students and their teachers, ran non-stop for three months.

For this pair of construction-savvy PCVs their favorite project was helping to build a three-story school halfway up El Cerro San Cristóbal, an enormous 1,200-foot-high dirt hill, completely bald, not even a weed except for a tall electrified cross standing at the very top to this very day.

Russo, a veritable workhorse, recalled the difficulty in pouring a cement roof halfway up the barren mountainside of El Cerro San Cristóbal:

FABRICA DE CEMENTO donated 300 bags of damaged cement. Was a tough job, not even a road from the highway out to El Cerro. Transported the bags to the bottom of the hill in a tractor trailer, sifted out the good cement, about 20% of each bag, and carried the good stuff up the hill by bucket. Normally, a cement truck pulls up and pours the cement and a roof is done in hours. But it took us three days to pour a cement roof on that school. It was a multi-generational PCV project. Six months after Leroy and I finished our tour of service, the school of El Cerro was finally finished, having required two generations of PCVs.

Next door was Rimac, Lima's oldest residential area, and behind Rimac was Plaza de Acho, oldest Spanish-built building in the New World. In Rimac, we're talking about neighborhoods almost 500 years old, going back to the early days of the Spanish conquest led by *Capitan* Francisco Pizarro and his bearded band of brothers, who arrived riding atop *caballos* (horses) and sporting "fire" arms.

El Cerro, an important *apu* (Inca sacred mountain), is one of Lima's oldest and most historic locales. In 1535, Francisco Pizarro's troops defeated a much larger Incan battalion coming down from Cusco. Shortly after the battle began, Inca military leaders were killed in combat in Rimac's narrow alleyways, causing their superior forces to retreat in panic. Pizarro gratefully named El Cerro after *San Cristóbal* (St. Christopher) Patron Saint of Travelers.

Remember, these dates do not include the communities and cultures who lived in Peru thousands of years before the Spanish arrived. That is not a typo; some researchers say sophisticated cultures existed in *Huaca Prieta*, along the north coast, 15,000 years ago.

Russo and Lange rented a simple, unadorned wooden house in Rimac, which became a watering hole for urban PCVs, a crash pad for wandering journalists, and an open door for interested Peruvians. Comparatively speaking, rural Andean PCVs worked at a glacial speed. Once the campesinos left for the fields, the town was as empty as a Western ghost town. On the other hand urban PCVs were busy every minute, as pervasive poverty seeped into their work and lives from all directions.

From Russo's worldview as a first generation American, he wanted his Peace Corps work to be the best for Peru and for the United States. To ensure that objective, he married a Peruvian. (And today they own homes in both countries. Lange, the architect, did the same thing. He returned to Minneapolis and became the City's Chief Architect. Soon Steve Russo was godfather to two of Leroy's children and vice versa.)

Young Volunteers talking about peace all day, working long weeks to achieve peace, eventually were rewarded with peace's dividend — love. In our Cornell group, six males and two females married Peruvians — 15% of our group. Several others,

I'm told, left lovers behind, "It was The Sixties," explained one still happily married PCV, "our hormones were raging."

Frequent visitors to Lange's and Russo's *tambo* (Inca rest stop) were the Comas co-op specialists PCVs Jerry Drake and Richard Welch (L.A. State Co-op 1964-66), and who were forming consumer co-ops in addition to working in the afternoons in downtown Lima at the Federation of Credit Cooperatives' headquarters.

When the word got out that Senator Kennedy wanted to see Comas and co-ops, Drake and Welch were ready; they had two consumer cooperatives lined up for the Senator to visit.

Jerry Drake, a lawyer recently admitted to the Missouri state bar, and Richard Welch from Rochester, New York, who was a Michigan State economics graduate, were, despite their youth, fully engaged. Their early pursuits in law and economics proved to be life-long. (Drake is still lawyering in Missouri; Welch is still teaching economics at University of Texas, San Antonio.)

The massive Comas barriada was a squalid, slapdash settlement of several hundred thousand Andean squatters, established in 1961 when they invaded vacant arid land outside Lima's city limits. Like other barriadas surrounding Lima, Comas had no amenities. No rain, no trees, no greenery, only sand and depleted dead dirt. All the surrounding brown hills were bald and bushless. No plumbing, disgusting open sewers, drinking water was brought in by truck.

Hundreds of thousands of these new Andean arrivals camped around the scabby edges of Lima, eking out a dire existence, living in flimsy structures made of bamboo poles and large estera mats. They survived on dried potatoes and chunks of fresh sugar cane, drank Inca Kola, smoked harsh Inca brand cigarettes, and, of course, some of them chewed coca leaves for energy and hunger suppression.

Chewing a wad of coca leaves was looked down upon by Peru's upper class. They believed it was something only *un indio* (Indigenous person) would do. Lima's polite society preferred chemically extracting their cocaine from the dark green coca leaf's highly nutritional binding elements, and then snorting it, using up far many more leaves than the Indigenous people ever chewed.

On November 12th RFK left for Comas with a contingent of Peace Corps, Embassy, and Peruvian government officials. D.J. and I followed, as did Russo in his press bus that carried 15 journalists.

There were many stops. Sometimes the journalists exited the bus, but often they stayed on board to take notes as Russo translated RFK's speeches while standing in the doorway of the bus.

Russo distinctly remembers a woman who sat behind the bus driver and never exited. He noticed what she had written and told her she was not getting the translation correct. "I don't care," she snapped back, "I'm going to write whatever I want."

Later Russo admitted in his rich New York Italian accent, "She made a lifelong impression upon me about da nature of joina-lism and da character of joina-lists." (Subsequently Russo would become President of NYC's Carpenters & Joiners Union Local #45.)

Leading the Comas caravan was Peace Corps' Associate Rep. "Jim" Lowry who supervised PCVs working in the barriadas. Formerly, Jim had been an Outward Bound instructor at Peace Corps' Camp Crozier in Puerto Rico, and he was on a first-name basis with Peace Corps/Washington's hierarchy who loved showcasing the jungle camps of Puerto Rico.

Not sure where Jim found the wheels, but he drove Senator Kennedy in a cool, turquoise-blue and white 1964 Chevy Impala convertible, top down. Kennedy stood most of the time waving to people as their convoy passed slowly through the crowded, decrepit streets of Lima, bursting at the seams with over two million desperate residents (eight million today).

Traveling with the Senator were Peru's U.S. AID Director William Dentzer and Peace Corps/Peru's Deputy Director Thorburn "Trip" Reid.

Trip was a classic Peace Corps senior staff person, smart and congenial. His charming manner matched his non-abrasive leadership style. A Harvard lawyer, he had been working for the ABA's (American Bar Association) World Peace in Law project when he heard the call of the New Frontier.

In 1962 he started working at Peace Corps/Washington in Charlie Peters' esteemed program evaluation unit, the only non-journalist of the team. Before taking on the job of Deputy Director in Peru, he had evaluated six Latin American projects, as well as projects in Senegal, Iran and Afghanistan. These were in-country studies that consisted of interviews that looked at training, and host country cooperation, and resulted in suggested programmatic improvements. His 1963 look at Bolivia's 120 PCVs, from four training groups, had taken three weeks and resulted in a 70-page, double-space analysis. Occupationally speaking it was nice road work for a globetrotter.

The plan was for Senator Kennedy to visit a cooperative.

Jerry Drake, a country boy raised in rural Western Missouri, had alerted the board of directors of the consumer cooperative at kilometer 11 of Senator Robert Kennedy's impending visit.

When RFK walked into the large room he boldly asked, in his high-pitched Bostonian accent, "*¿Que pasa aqui?*" (What's going on here?) Drake introduced Senator Kennedy to each of the seven board members of the consumer cooperative shaking each man's hand.

One of their members, Mario Castro Castro, gave an eloquent speech about cooperatives and cooperacíon. Peru's intelligentsia had decided, as a defense against becoming embroiled in the Cold War — having to side with either Capitalism or Communism — to choose a third rail, *Cooperativísmo* — an economic model based in part on the Incan practice of mit'a.

After watching Mario deliver the powerful message to Kennedy, PCVs Drake and Welch both felt Kennedy had been shortchanged by the Embassy translator, "*Desgraciadamente* (Unfortunately) much was lost in translation."

Kennedy then walked across the plaza to Iglesia Santiago Apostol (Catholic Church of Apostle James) to visit Father Bill

Francis, nephew of Boston's Cardinal Cushing, who ran a vigorous community services outreach operation.

Behind the church stood a short row of one-story cement-block buildings, and when space for a community project was needed the annex was used. One building was used to store kerosene, another one Jerry used to organize a consumer co-op. Life in the teeming barriada was a day-to-day improvisation.

After leaving the church, RFK came upon a small estera hut belonging to an Andean family and went inside where he remained for a considerable time.

Drake recalled the incident:

My compadres in the cooperative movement were VERY impressed. I remember the excited talk and the observation that a Peruvian politician would never do that. The President of the cooperative, Manual Mora, took me by the arm, pulled me aside, and whispered, "*Estados Unidos es muy democratico. demasiado democratico.*" ("United States is very democratic, too democratic.")

Kennedy and his entourage then circled behind Iglesia Santiago Apostol and began investigating the small cement-block buildings.

The only photo I took of RFK was at the co-op annex. As he entered, I caught the Senator reaching up to a youngster hanging off the rooftop.

That spontaneous connection instantly produced smiles on everyone's face, including the Senator's. It was an example of many scenes to follow where RFK purposely reached out to connect with young children. They were his number one concern wherever he traveled. His aide and longtime friend William vanden Heuvel believed RFK's affinity for children was because they had no power to protect themselves. They were the ultimate underdog, a fact that had nothing to do with their race, color, or creed.

RFK in the Comas barriada, Santiago Apostol Church Co-op Annex, Lima Peru, Nov. 12, 1965. L-R William Dentzer, Peru AID director; unidentified Peruvian; Willam vanden Heuvel, Kennedy aide; unidentified Peruvian government official; RFK; Jim Lowry, Peace Corps/Lima Rep.; unidentified woman. *Photo by PCV Sweet William. Photo Restoration by Publisher Marian Haley Beil*

RFK had been visibly moved by the filth Comas families had to live with. This was not the first time he had seen revolting conditions. During his Senate sub-committee investigations he had seen gross poverty up close and personal, from the Deep South to the American Heartland, from Pine Ridge to West Virginia. Child poverty rang Robert Kennedy's alarm bell wherever he went.

As the caravan left Comas, Senator Kennedy asked the AID Director William Dentzer about the U.S. helping Comas improve its water system, "So they don't have to rely on trucks to deliver their drinking water."

The AID director stammered, cleared his throat as if he was going to speak, but then no words came out.

Suddenly, Dentzer changed the subject and asked what was their ETA for the San Martin de Porres barriada.

RFK repeated, "How can we get a water system up and running for the people of Comas?"

There was no answer.

The AID director looked straight ahead, bureaucratically hogtied by the President of the United States.

(Today there is a street in Comas that bears Robert Kennedy's name.)

The greeting at San Martin de Porres barriada was overwhelming and exuberant.

Again, they were flooded with love and enthusiasm. Desert brown dust from the caravan covered everyone. Children dressed in khaki school uniforms ran everywhere, gleefully screaming, "Ken-ah-dee, Ken-ah-dee." Thousands circled the vehicles. Brass trumpets brashly announced their arrival, Andean harps were strummed passionately, bass drummers never stopped beating — it was a barriada hoedown.

Later in the afternoon, D.J. and I went to a press conference that Senator Kennedy held at the downtown Hotel Bolivar where he and his entourage were guests.

In between sipping frothy Pisco Sours — Lima's best, I asked Richard Goodwin whether the Senator could help loosen up AID funds for the Mantaro Valley's electric cooperative that PCVs were working on. Since arriving in the fall of 1964 we had been helping communities sign up socios (members), to stockpile eucalyptus trees for light poles, and to map out house-to-house installation networks.

Goodwin said there was nothing they could do.

Standing outside the press conference, RFK's two Senate aides, Tom Johnson and Adam Walinsky, asked D.J. and me to "cover" a speech for RFK. He would not be able to attend a scheduled afternoon meeting with students at the University of San Martin de Porres, a new Catholic university (named for Peru's sole Black Saint), and "personally convey his regrets."

We were happy to comply.

When we arrived at the university, several hundred cheering students met us. It was soon apparent to everyone in the auditorium that although we were short-haired gringos in coat and ties, we were the wrong gringos.

D.J. was born and raised in rural eastern Iowa, blond and naturally humorous, an Iowa State alum, and was considered an ideal John Deere Company recruit; and I was a pink-faced New Yorker, a former Santa Fe switchman from blue-collar Berdoo on a two-year government-paid honeymoon. We were clean-shaven and rosy-cheeked; we even dressed like we were part of the Kennedy team.

After we conveyed the Senator's regrets, several students disappointedly gave us letters to pass on to the Senator as we made a fast exit out on to the street. (The John F. Kennedy Presidential Library Archives still possess those letters.)

That evening the hottest ticket in Lima was an invitation to the U.S. Ambassador's Reception for Senator Robert Kennedy and his entourage of family, friends, and news reporters. Anybody who was somebody would be there. Lima, Spain's Vice Royalty for over 275 years, still possessed some of the world's wealthiest families. The Kennedys were America's gold and Peru's upper class wanted their time to appraise them.

Obviously, no PCVs were allowed to attend or 400 hungry young Americans would have descended upon Lima's exclusive San Ysidro neighborhood and attacked the Ambassador's Party like starving locusts.

D.J. and I, though, were working in a semi-official capacity and were able to convince the Marine Security detail that we had to report back to RFK's aides who were "inside the Ambassador's party."

There we were, country bumpkins from the primitive Andes, hobnobbing at the Ambassador's deluxe social affair, rubbing elbows with Lima's *gente decente*, scarfing down delicious hors d'oeuvres, sipping Crystal sparkling champagne.

Across the floor D.J. and I spotted Ethel Kennedy talking with El Cordobés, whose exceptional reflexes and raw courage led him to world prominence that made him the inspiration for books and song. He was, also, one handsome dude.

Moments before introducing ourselves to Ethel and El Cordobés, senior Peace Corps staff detected our pauper presence. Trip Reid may have thought we were going to speak to Ethel, but actually we were angling to speak with El Cordobés. We wanted to show him a new bull fighting "pass" we had seen in the *sierra* (mountains) that campesinos called *El Condor pasa*.

But, no, the history of bullfighting was denied that innovation because the authorities threw us out before we could impart our high altitude discovery to El Cordobés.

As soon as Trip saw us and our country boots, he took direct action and escorted us, *"personalmente,"* out of the party and on to the cobblestoned street — the letters for RFK were handed off just before we were whisked through the massive wrought-iron gates of the Ambassador's resplendent residence.

Our sudden departure may have appeared embarrassing to some, but to PCVs who lived in rural Peru, far from Lima and its fancy flush toilets, our momentary penetration into their regal splendor was a daring invasion by *los serranos*.

Everybody wanted to meet RFK, and RFK wanted to meet everybody. It was only a question of scheduling. He was a curious man who took advantage of the intellectual resources around him; and like his brother, the President, he didn't suffer fools. He wanted to meet with political players, activists, artists and publishers.

After the Ambassador's Reception he had scheduled a dinner with five university student activists who had received printed dinner invitations to privately meet and eat with RFK at the Ambassador's residence. Joining the five prominent student activists were two important Peruvian publishers; one was 68-year-old Pedro Beltran, respected publisher of La Prensa, and the other was 28-year-old Manuel D'Ornellas, new op-ed editor of the daily Expreso whose founders had recently helped engineer Belaúnde's 1963 Presidential victory.

It was a closed meeting with RFK for seven influential and politically savvy Peruvians: "*la entrevista para los siete*" — (Interview for Seven.) They were excited to be meeting JFK's brother, but why was the bullfighter El Cordobés present?

It was a question asked by the student activists as they sat down for dinner on the 12th of November 1965. (Alfredo Filomeño J., one of those five students, 50 years later in his 2015 blog, *Politica del 60 al 90*, would repeat that question to no avail.)

Besides a similarity in their hairstyles, the Peruvian political intelligentsia never figured out what a rich American politician had in common with a famous Spanish bullfighter. Both men were slight in height and high on the international paparazzi Hot List.

A close examination of how they dealt with life's disappointments reveals their common strategy for coping. Fearlessly living in the present, possessing a quick sense of humor, and their willingness to die for their causes, these were attributes they had in common.

Robert Kennedy's wondrous, but tragic journey through life, and what that did and didn't do to him, are subjects ripe for speculation. How could anyone go through such pain and suffering, all in the public's eye, and supposedly never cry? One thing that definitely appears in his life, post-11/22/63, is his fearlessness. After fate ripped away his older brother, whom he had passionately served, RFK was now on his own, much like the orphaned El Cordobés, both riding the unpredictable rapids of life. Their meeting at the Ambassador's Reception sparked an immediate friendship. Naturally and spontaneously RFK dragged El Cordobés into "*la entrevista para los siete.*"

Those who wonder whether RFK was as fearless as El Cordobes should know that when RFK and his entourage were in Northeastern Brazil, at the end of their journey, on the way back to the U.S. they took a side trip to Manaus, the Amazon River's biggest port, where Richard Goodwin and the Senator took a side trip to go swimming in a tributary of the Amazon River infested with aggressive flesh-eating piraña.

As the Senator dove in, he reasoned with Goodwin, "Piraña have never been known to bite a U.S. Senator."

7

THE CUSCO CONSPIRACY

Traveling through the Andes with the Senator's entourage, *Washington Post* reporter Dan Kurzman filed his exposé, "Peace Corpsmen in Peru Attack U.S. Aid Policy," (see "Heavy Media" on page 251) a news story that revealed that the freeze of AID funds in Peru was due to the IPC dispute, a fact that had been uncovered during Senator Kennedy's visit with Peace Corps Volunteers working in the Cusco region. That story wasn't published until November 14th, the day after RFK and company left Peru for Chile. Oddly enough the *Washington Post* said the Senator's Thursday November 11th visit happened Saturday, November 13th, which was just one of many fabrications the exposé contained.

As soon as the Sunday November 14 newspaper arrived at the Oval Office, Peace Corps Director Sargent Shriver was on the carpet apologizing to LBJ and explaining his new preventative measures for keeping the Peace Corps out of politics. Sarge's apologies immediately ran downhill to Assistant Secretary of State for Latin America Jack Vaughn, U.S. Ambassador to Peru J. Wesley Jones and, finally, for exposing the President's policy of corporate favoritism, Peace Corps/Peru's Deputy Director Trip Reid received Shriver's personal tidings before noon. Shriver knew all the evaluators and valued them highly.

In answering Kurzman's questions at the Turista Hotel in Cusco, where Senator Kennedy was hosting a dinner for the three PCVs from Compone, Trip was forced to admit the uncomfortable fact. Yes, IPC, a Rockefeller family-owned oil company, was in a dispute with the Peruvian government about how to split the profits in their new contract. . . . and that's what was holding up important Alliance for Progress development funds.

Ironically, of all the people who knew of AID's freeze on funds being tied to the IPC contract dispute, it was, according to the *Washington Post,* JFK's Peace Corps who stood tallest. In an old-fashioned example of speaking truth to power, Peace Corps Volunteers and staff forced the President's hand by making the IPC controversy public during RFK's visit to Cusco. So said the *Post* news story . . . not the facts of RFK's visit.

From President Belaúnde on down, everyone told him about the IPC dispute and long before he got to Cusco. When he went to Compone the staircase he stood on had just been completed through a community faena in time for the Senator's arrival, not long delayed by the AID funding freeze, as Kurzman's alleged "PCV" asserted in an unnamed community. The fabrications were designed to disguise where and who was involved, according to Kurzman's exposé.

A conspiracy had definitely occurred that November 11th night in Cusco at the Turista Hotel. Richard Goodwin and his colleagues' plan to expose LBJ's failure to back up the promises of the Alliance for Progress had worked. Sadly, the facts revealed that the ugly Americans had returned to power.

No one in Peru knew of the uproar Senator Robert Kennedy's visit and its press coverage had caused President Johnson and his State Department. Everyone in Peru already knew about the IPC dispute holding up AID funding, a fact LBJ had hoped could be kept secret from the American public. Now with his perfidy exposed, the government had to set in motion forces to contravene the damning disclosure.

W.W. Rostow, LBJ's National Security Advisor, had previously warned the President of the need to release some "soft funds." The front cover photo of Peru's popular *Caretas* Magazine's April 1965 issue had featured a fearsome group of *guerrilleros* wearing black leather jackets, black berets and toting machine-guns, operating somewhere in *la montaña*, the Amazon Rainforest side of the Andes, which is not exactly the place you'd wear a leather jacket.

After Senator Kennedy's departure from Peru, Rostow examined potential prospects in Peru for funding. In a December 6th cable, he supported Ambassador Jones' judgment that the "rural electric cooperative was a Peace Corps project;" Asst. Secretary Vaughn was of the same mind.

The year before, on December, 6, 1964, Marie and I had met Walt Whitman Rostow. In Lima for an Inter-American conference, Rostow and some colleagues had taken the train to Huancayo to see the Sunday Silent Fair. It was there that we ran into him.

Non-native tourists stood out amongst the thousands of shoppers because of their height. Inca descendants, wearing rubber-tire sandals, average 5'4" in height.

I recognized him and introduced him to Marie. He responded to her puzzlement by famously joking, "You don't have to know who I am."

In the fall of 1962, I had taken a political science seminar at UCLA titled "Nuclear Defense Strategies," and we all knew who Walt Rostow was. He was author of a bold new theory presented in his book, *The Stages of Economic Growth: A Non-Communist Manifesto* that endeared him to the Kennedy Administration that planned to promote international economic development in places where Colonialism was being ousted.

Dr. Rostow was not just an intellectual.

During W.W. II, his job was targeting industrial sites in the bombing war against Germany. As a consequence, he became a gung-ho pro-war advisor to both Kennedy and Johnson, famously creating "Operation Rolling Thunder" (March 2, 1965–November 2, 1968), the most intense air/ground battle of the Cold War: American air power vs. Communist supplied surface-to-air missile defense systems. Rostow was an academic gone ballistic. Of the many books exploring his legacy, the one that captured him best was Daniel Milne's *America's Rasputin*.

We ate lunch together at the Olímpico Restaurante during which Walt asked us about our work, and generously picked up the tab.

Having learned from my UCLA seminar that nuclear escalation policies would govern our growing military involvement in Vietnam, I sent Dr. Rostow a postcard over the holidays, questioning whether our activities in Vietnam would inevitability lead to the use of nuclear weapons.

The whole world wanted the answer to that question.

Although we were on a first name basis, I never heard back from Walt. No holiday card. Nothing. Yet it is evident that Dr. Rostow's first-hand knowledge of the Mantaro Valley was a key factor in determining the electric co-op's destiny.

I was in Lima for the mid-January, 1966 Graduate Record Exams being given at the Embassy when I heard that the Ambassador and our new country director, Eugene Baird, would be driving up to La Oroya in the Ambassador's big black Chevy Suburban.

Baird, a bright and energetic new leader, added long-legged me to the January 21, 1966 manifest so I could lobby the Ambassador on the Mantaro Valley electric co-op. As we drove up into the Andes following the Rimac river valley, Baird tossed me one softball after another, "Guillermo (William), tell the Ambassador why the electric cooperative is a good use of foreign aid. What's the electric co-op's biggest problem today?" Eventually the Ambassador conceded, "Funding would probably occur in June."

Good luck passing that story around!

The U.S. government's word regarding promised aid wasn't worth much in Peru. Naturally no one on the ground in Peru knew of W.W. Rostow's involvement; those types of details appear decades later when researchers track down who caused the death of JFK's revolutionary Alliance for Progress.

Naturally, on such a long journey, I eventually pushed open the envelope of cordiality too far. I asked the Ambassador his opinion of the previous year's non-fiction best-seller The Invisible Government, an exposé by David Wise about the CIA's role in foreign policy — the coups in Guatemala (Operation PBSUCCESS) and Iran (Operation Ajax) and the Bay of Pigs operation.

Ambassador Jones reticently responded, "It's a shame a book like that was written when our government was locked in such a serious struggle."

I didn't know if he was referring to the Cold War or the Vietnam War. I was surprised that even in an intimate setting of a large Chevy Suburban, far from civilization, he clammed up.

Little did anyone know at the time that the CIA, according to the Pentagon Papers (1971), was the main force behind expanding the American role in the Vietnam War from advisory to adversarial.

At Morochocha's 15,000-foot-high poly-metallic mines — copper, gold, silver, lead — the mining supervisor happily greeted the ambassador's vehicle with a wooden box filled with his respects. At La Oroya, when I got out to catch a ride to Huancayo, I was given a slab of amethyst crystals from the Casapalca Mine.

Later I learned that miners traditionally give newcomers a mineralized gift.

Two days later, Ambassador Jones and Country Director Baird visited the Peace Corps' Huancayo office where again Volunteers lobbied for the Mantaro Valley's electric co-op.

Michael Heyn from Manzanares spoke for all of us as he eloquently argued how electricity would transform one of Peru's great agricultural centers. ("Manzanares' Miguel" — Michael — went on to a forty-year career with the United Nations making many such arguments.)

In March of 1966, Walt Rostow turned the National Security screws and convinced LBJ to fund two projects:

1) President Belaúnde's new community action agency *Cooperación Popular*, and

2) Mantaro Valley's rural electric cooperative #127.

(Mantaro Valley Electric Cooperative #127 was inaugurated in Huancayo July 23, 1970, as an official component of Peru's national electric grid.)

As Harvard Dean McGeorge Bundy had warned, Ambassador Jones, following a "three-month delay," announced funding June 21, 1966.

For the Cusco conspirators, using the Peace Corps as their foil did not fool the dean. Even so, any activist would agree that a three-month wait was a small indignation to pay for funding two exemplary, multi-million dollar projects that directly aided the poor of Peru.

Although it was not their intention, by "outing LBJ" the Cusco conspirators had forced him to finance two important consequential projects for Peru, one for the present, one for the future. IPC's dispute remained unresolved, eventually leading to a military overthrow in October 1968.

Wherever Kennedy appeared in Peru, the public mobbed him, even in the remote corners of the Andes. It was as if they knew his destiny. They were pulling him back on to the world stage to take over his brother's leadership of the New Frontier; and even more urgently, to stop a war that was dividing America as if the Civil War had been reignited. Kennedy's trip through Latin America was such a positive experience he asked Mankiewicz to become his Press Secretary.

Following the trip, whatever Kennedy did the media recorded his every act.

LBJ dreaded his every step and frequently went in the opposite direction. In April of 1965, to demonstrate his indifference to JFK's Alliance for Progress and its prescribed social reforms, LBJ had ordered an old-school style U.S. Marine invasion of the Dominican Republic over suspected Communists in the newly elected government, several of whom it was later discovered were long deceased.

To make his opposition to LBJ official and permanent, RFK's May 9-10, 1966 speech to the U.S. Senate: "The Alliance for Progress: Symbol & Substance," reported on what he had learned from the November 1965 trip to Latin America. Passionately he described the area's vast potential and how its historic problems were entwined with our own.

In summary, he offered, "Eight economic development answers: #1 continue immeasurable work done by the Peace Corps,

#2 product diversification, #3 responsible private investment."
And there at #4, RFK put into the Congressional Record a new
standard to prevent any more IPC type disputes from impeding
social progress . . . "#4 by discarding the practice of using aid
programs to insure any form of special treatment for American
companies."

To add salt to the wound of LBJ's caustic policies, RFK reminded the Senate that during the period when aid was shut-
down in Peru, "Military assistance doubled from $5.2M to
$10M, more than any other Latin American nation. Our poli-
cymakers may not have intended this result, but I am sure that
many Peruvians thought we favored arms over social reform."

In closing, he reminded his fellow Senators, "The best coun-
terinsurgency is social and political progress." His Senate speech
was a fitting tribute to his brother's noble experiment; it also
exposed who trashed it.

One wonders, had JFK's noble experiment, Alianza para el Progreso, been allowed to succeed, would our southern border be as
swamped as it is today with thousands of people fleeing bank-
rupt countries, cartel-controlled economies, communities in violent revolt — desperate citizens faced with the dire choices of
either death or departure?

8

RFK'S WAR ON POVERTY

The November 1965 trip to Latin America had deeply affected Robert Kennedy. The impoverished barriadas of Lima, and the grotesque favelas of Rio de Janeiro, were travesties of modern life, as were the urban ghettos of America. These human calamities stirred within him the desire to try to solve the intractable multi-faceted problem of urban poverty. The trip had given him some ideas to use in focusing a programmatic attack. No doubt he read Mankiewicz's provocative community development strategy: "Peace Corps: A Revolutionary Force." He saw for himself how the Peace Corps and U.S AID had successfully employed the concept of community development, long a tool in rural America.

By February 1966, RFK had amassed a sizeable force of businessmen and activists dedicated to revitalizing urban neighborhoods instead of destroying them. Wall Street bankers, Ford Foundation executives, and local community activists were part and parcel of Robert Kennedy's community development program destined for a black ghetto in the heart of Brooklyn, New York.

Peace Corps' founding Director, Sargent Shriver, had begun working for Joseph P. Kennedy — father of JFK and RFK — shortly after WWII, helping to run his newly purchased Chicago Merchandise Mart, once the world's largest office building. After his 1953 marriage to JFK's sister, Eunice, he also began serving as President of Chicago's Department of Education in 1955. As a consequence, Shriver developed strong ideas about making bureaucracies more effective and less boring.

In creating a new bureaucracy for the Peace Corps and its civilian Volunteers in 1961, Shriver specified that a person could only work at the agency for five years. This famous "In-Up-Out" policy roiled traditional government bureaucrats. The five-year limit meant you couldn't get stale. After five years, you had to go somewhere else for five years before returning for another tour. The rule was also designed to keep the organization free of bureaucracy's many stagnating features, i.e., don't rock the boat.

At the fifth anniversary of the signing of the Peace Corps' Executive Order #10924 on March 1, 1961, "Sarge" set the example and resigned. Immediately, he took on management of LBJ's new Office of Economic Opportunity (OEO) — the War on Poverty. Trip Reid left the Peace Corps in 1966 for OEO.

Jack Hood Vaughn, no doubt chafing under Thomas Mann's impossible Doctrine, happily left the State Department to run the Peace Corps as its 2nd Director. Jack's no-brainer comment to Congress lived long after he did, "Peace is cheaper than war."

To be in closer contact with the issue of poverty, the new Senator from New York requested being assigned to two Labor Department related Sub-Committees: Manpower, Employment & Poverty and Migratory Workers.

It was not surprising that when United Auto Workers' (UAW) President Walter Reuther called, Senator Kennedy personally answered. Reuther had been an early and enthusiastic supporter of JFK's 1960 Presidential campaign. Reuther, who founded the UAW in 1946, was America's most prominent labor leader. He knew getting the mob out of union life would only add more members, which could be cashed in the world of elective politics.

Reuther had impressive credentials. He had galvanized the union movement of the 1930s and had organized and led the UAW into becoming America's most progressive union. He championed workers' rights, as well as civil rights, women's rights, even environmental regulation. Since the 1930s, Walter Reuther believed the lowly migrant farmworker could be organized. Robert Kennedy, he believed, was a logical person to champion so desperate a cause.

In his call to Senator Kennedy, Reuther explained that he had just admitted a new union into the AFL-CIO combine: National Farm Workers (NFW). In his recent trip to San Francisco, Reuther had gone to the Central Valley and met their leaders, César Chávez and Dolores Huerta. "They're organizing a farmworkers union," Reuther reported, "while holding a strike against table grape growers."

Paul Schrade, Reuther's Assistant, had worked closely with Senator Kennedy's legislative aide Peter Edelman in advancing the farmworker cause. The Senate Migratory Workers Sub-Committee had scheduled hearings in mid-March for Delano, the very heart of the immense San Joaquin Valley agricultural complex. It would be a providential moment for the Senator and for the Latino community.

Senate committee hearings were old hat for Robert Kennedy. In the early 1950s, after graduating from Virginia Law School, he went to work for his new father-in-law's good friend, U.S. Senator Joe McCarthy of Wisconsin.

By 1957 Kennedy was working as chief council for the Senate Select Committee on Improper Union & Management activities — dubbed the McClelland Committee — where he acquired his investigative experiences.

Now, in the spring of 1966, he was acting at the behest of Walter Reuther, America's working-class leader.

Flying cross-country the Senator arrived in time for the last day's testimonies. He began to ratchet up his concerns by grilling the local sheriff as to why he arrested 44 of Chávez's protesters who had not broken any law. The Sheriff of Kern County argued it was a preventative measure. Senator Kennedy strongly suggested during the lunch break that both the Sheriff and the District Attorney read the U.S. Constitution.

9

THE GREAT CHILEAN JEWELRY HEIST

Our Peace Corps service ended on June 6ᵗʰ, 1966.

Sicaya's leadership hosted a May 31, 1966 *Despedida* (Farewell) for
Guillermo and Marie at Las Brisas (Breezes) del Mantaro Restaurant.
Because the Volunteers promoted cooperatives and because they pro-
duced no children during their two years, Guillermo was re-named,
*El Presidente de la cooperativa de los Inproductivos. Photo by Marie
Evensen*

That was two weeks before Ambassador Jones announced funding
for a project I had worked on throughout my two-year assignment. I never knew of the electric cooperative's success until 52
years later when Gonzalo Romero Sommer, writing his Ph.D.
dissertation about Peru's first rural electric co-op, found me.

To think of the long Mantaro River Valley, source of the Amazon River, generating electric light does bring forth a smile of
satisfaction. This is the type of delayed gratification every Peace
Corps Volunteer relishes — proof our work did good. America

was there in the Andes helping Peru's poor light their pathway into modern times.

None the wiser of the AID funding, we left Peru and turned south for Chile.

There was reason for us to go to Chile.

A small miracle had occurred. One of our suitcase's had been stolen while we were on a vacation to Chile the previous February, and it had been returned to the U.S. Embassy in Santiago with some items, and we were going to collect them.

We couldn't imagine what had been returned: Marie's jewelry? our 35 mm camera? her sweaters? my undies?

Back in February, when we had needed a break from the crushingly slow life of Andean poverty and the timelessness of rural life, we decided to visit Chile. Chile, a narrow (217 miles wide), long (2,653 miles) country that had no Indigenous peoples, no Amazon Rainforest, the world's largest salt lick, 1,500 miles of white sandy beaches where, in the bone-dry north coast, it doesn't rain for centuries.

Our neighbors, the Heyns, graduates of Stanford and San Jose State, gave Chile their Palo Alto stamp of approval.

Having been raised by a family of modest net worth, our February trip was frugal in its design.

We flew from Lima on Fawcett Airlines in a vintage DC-3 to Tacna on Peru's southern border with Chile.

Then we took a cab across the border to the Chilean airport in Arica where we boarded a modern LAN Chile DC-6 bound for Santiago, thereby eliminating the higher cost of international travel.

As we boarded, a blonde-haired blue-eyed stewardess greeted us. I immediately went into culture shock. She claimed to be German, which did not surprise us. At The Balkan restaurant in Lima, our favorite eatery when we went to the city, we heard German immigrants, who looked much like her, singing nostal-

gic songs of their homeland like "Wieder Verliebt" ("Falling in
Love Again"), and enjoyed *Kartoffelsalat* (German potato salad)
and *wiener schnitzel* (breaded, pan-fried veal cutlet).

No, our stewardess was not a newly arrived German; she said
she was 5th generation.

Immigrant Germans in 1851 had founded Chile's most
southern city, Puerto Montt, the last port before reaching the
rugged Patagonian archipelago.

After surviving the horrendous experience of rounding Cape
Horn — southern-most tip of South America — on their
months-long treks from Europe to California's goldfields, some
German immigrants lost their gold fever and declared, "First
sight of solid land, we're going no further." Those European adventurers settled southern Chile.

From Santiago, the capitol of Chile, we took Meiggs' first train
line to Valparaiso, on the coast, and stayed in Viña del Mar, an
upscale seaside resort with its own casino, a replica of Catalina
Island's casino. We took the train from Concepción inland to
the Lake District and south to Puerto Montt, an eight-hour
journey that stopped in every city, like a local with passengers
quickly getting on and off. Luggage was stored in the small area
between the entrance and the seating area of each car.

We passed through the city of Osorno, named for 8,701 foot
Mt. Osorno, South America's Mt. Fuji — one of the many post-
card-perfect snow-covered volcanoes that dot the spine of the
Andes as they run south through Chile into Patagonia. Osorno looked like an ordinary city with streetlights and sidewalks,
parks and curbs; it had crooks as well.

Two young men in their twenties boarded the train in Osorno, seated themselves in our car, and then at the next stop
suddenly got off. After the train left the station I checked our
bags and our blue suitcase with clothes, sweaters, camera, and
Marie's jewelry bag, which contained an exquisite silver filigree
necklace made of tiny silver globes, silver llama earrings, and
silver bracelets, was gone. A disaster. I was furious. A perfect

gambit, they knew we wouldn't get off the train until our final stop.

Puerto Montt looked like I imagined the Swiss Alps would look like. Everything was clean and green, manicured and delineated precisely. There was easy access to apple strudel pastries, Mercedes-Benz buses, and no one defecating in the streets. Even the commercials, before the local movie started, promoted Flying Lufthansa.

The robbers did not know we were Peace Corps Volunteers but I still felt indignant. I was not an ugly American. I was a financially embarrassed working class American and I couldn't afford this loss. I wanted to get our goods back, which meant I was going to return to the scene of the crime.

I hopped on the next bus heading north.

In Osorno I went to the police station, filed a robbery report, went to the train station and did the same. Then I went to the local newspaper and bought a small personal ad in the Spanish language newspaper — chastising the robbers in Spanish for stealing our memories of Peru, telling them we were Peace Corps Volunteers, demanding our goods be returned, and that we could be reached through the American Embassy in Santiago.

At least I felt better, riding the smooth Benz bus ride back to Puerto Montt. Strauss waltzes absorbed my angst. The gorgeous countryside and its lush farmlands were another world far from impoverished Indigenous Peru.

During our June 6th final debriefing by the Peace Corps, Marie and I received a message from the U.S. Embassy in Santiago: someone had returned our blue suitcase, which contained "some items."

The first stop on our tour of southern South American on our way home, contained a surprise gift being returned four months later by whom and why. I guess this is an example of where persistence paid off, but that's about all I can take credit for.

The broken-into suitcase contained two things: our Argus C-3 35mm camera — our film having been removed — and

Marie's jewelry bag — and none of the jewels were missing! They kept her sweaters and my undies.

Throughout my life I have recovered stolen and lost items by not giving up on them, although I must admit persistence hasn't helped recover lost opportunities.

10

THE LONG WAY HOME

For a working-class guy of average intelligence with no endowments other than the ability to question authority, this trip home to California via a tour of South America was a rare opportunity to see the New World on the government's dime. Peace Corps shipped our goods to California, and gave us Pan Am tickets from Rio de Janeiro to NYC.

After suffering Peru's crude and scary transit options for nearly two years, our trip would be, comparatively speaking, a luxurious experience.

Streaking over the Andes from Santiago to Mendoza, Argentina in a sleek French Mirage jet, serenely passing by snow-capped 22,835-foot Mt. Aconcagua, tallest mountain of the Western Hemisphere; relaxing aboard a *lujo* (luxury), air-conditioned double-decker bus, cruising comfortably across the Argentine *pampa* listening to Mozart, sipping cognac courtesy of the bus company ... all overwhelming.

It was a very far cry from the squawking chickens and vomiting children aboard a small, cramped Andean bus built on top of a flatbed truck with narrow seats that were so small I had to ride sidesaddle for hours on end. Not to mention, Andean bus crashes were the biggest killer of Peruvian adults. A loaded bus going off an Andean road in the sheer-sided mountains rolled so far there were never any survivors.

Cosmopolitan Buenos Aires spoke its snooty Castilian Spanish with an Italian accent.

Every afternoon at 4 p.m. they religiously celebrated "*once*" (pronounced OWN-say, meaning the number 11) by drinking a *copita de aguardiente*. So named "once" for aguardiente's (schnapps) eleven letters. It was a stilted tradition that for Marie and me was slightly interrupted by a military overthrow of the government that very afternoon we were there (June 28,1966).

Everyone is so polite in Argentina. White gloves and gray vicuña shawls, very Victorian in a Northern Italian sort of way. Of course we went to the Teatro Colón, one of the world's 10 best opera houses — the vertiginous 6th balcony.

Tiny Paraguay is a jungle outpost, whose backdoor leads into the dark unknown of the Amazon's *mato grosso* where in 1925 English explorer Percy Fawcett went missing searching for the mythical Lost City of Z.

The country was ruled by military dictator General Alfredo Stroessner, whose tyrannical tenure lasted 35 years: 1954–1989. Its Indigenous people speak Guaraní, women vendors in the outdoor markets smoke cigars, and Paraguayan boy-soldiers guard the Presidential Palace, descendants of Paraguay's 1864-1870 suicidal war against the Triple Alliance of Argentina, the Empire of Brazil, and newly formed Uruguay.

During that war, President Francisco Lopez II and his Irish born wife Eliza's chilling battle cry: "No Prisoners — No Surrender," had almost proven fatal, killing 70% of Paraguay's adult population and 96% of their adult male population!

Paraguay's six-year battle to end slavery was brutally crushed by Brazil's overwhelming army of illiterate slave-soldiers who were handsomely paid by Portuguese slavers to fight Paraguay.

If one were to ever be jailed in Paraguay, there was a certain hell to pay. Rumors abounded that prisoners were forced to impregnate three Paraguayan women before being released. Long prison terms, coupled with frequent conjugal visits, were Paraguay's criminal justice norms.

From Paraguay's magnificent Iguaçu Falls, it is a short flight to sprawling São Paulo, Brazil, the Western Hemisphere's second largest city with six million people living in the metropolitan area (22 million today ... Western Hemisphere's largest city). São Paulo was modern and friendly, its jazz bands played till dawn.

Up the coast, on a 222-mile jet flight, was elegant Rio de Janeiro, former 18th-century capital of Portugal's slave-based Brazilian colony. Surrounded by impoverished favelas, much like Lima and its wretched barriadas, Rio was the heart of romantic Brazil; Ipanema Beach, and its trippy Copacabana oceanfront walkway, its glittering tiara.

As we lazily walked along Copacabana's celebrated Promenade we ran into a *Time Magazine* correspondent we had met in Huancayo. He was the reporter who the previous August had written an overly-imagined story about *los guerrilleros* in the Central Andes of Peru saying that ". . . Huancayo swarms with soldiers and military vehicles." (see *Heavy Media* on page 249)

We had eaten dinner with him one evening at La Turista Hotel in Huancayo, and spent three hours together as he assembled the facts of his story, which were: Nothing going on other than a military DC-3 transport had landed in Juaja, 28 miles away.

As soon as I recognized him, I stopped him and popped the question: "Where did those military vehicles come from?" Sheepishly, he explained *Time* editors had received "classified" information, which could color a story's outcome that we on the scene "can't fully see."

Sensing an opportunity to parlay his awkwardness into an insight on media life, I pressed him. And it was there, on Copacabana's dazzling sunny walkway, we learned that *Commentary Magazine* contributor Norman Gall, who had been hanging around the Peace Corps office in Huancayo for over a year, supposedly writing a story for *Saturday Evening Post Magazine* about Colombian and Peruvian guerrilla movements, was also "a stringer for the CIA."

Thrilled to be warm and not having to wear sweaters and scarves, we went in shorts and shirt sleeves to see Maracaña Stadium, South America's largest soccer stadium — gigantic, electric-blue and spaceship-shaped — that had held 200,000 futbol (soccer) fans for its opening competition, the 1950 World Cup.

Stadium vendors were selling poster-sized photos of Brazilian soccer star Pelé with RFK celebrating together after his November 21st match the previous fall, when Brazil tied the Russians 2-2. Looking at their happy locker room photograph you couldn't help but smile too.

Pelé and RFK 11/21/1965

It was obvious that RFK had received in Brazil the same enthusiastic embrace he had received in Peru.

The day after meeting Pelé was the 2nd Anniversary of JFK's murder — RFK and company flew to Northeastern Brazil where Portugal's almost 500-year-long colony, financed on the backs of African slaves, had long dominated the landscape producing white sugar for the world. There appeared to be no overt racism; African descendants moved freely in and about Brazilian society but not vertically into the upper echelons. In the coastal town of Natal, RFK and Ethel went to Mass at a small church. Later, he gave the Governor's Speech at the new *Instituto de educacáo superior Presidente Kennedy* and spoke to 100,000 cheering Brazilians in no uncertain terms about the coming revolution:

> THE RESPONSIBILITY of our time is nothing less than to lead a revolution, a revolution which will be peaceful if we are wise enough, humane if we care, successful if we are fortunate enough, but a revolution which will come whether we will it or not. We can affect its character; we cannot alter its inevitability.

Next day, the entourage traveled down the coast to Recife, where Brazil is only 1,100 miles from Dakar, Senegal, Africa. Recife was the New World's first slave port, founded in 1537.

The Senator gave his well-honed student speech "Freedom and Justice" to a boisterous throng of thousands of university students, their out-stretched arms reaching forward as if in a mass salute. It wasn't hard for *latinoamericanos* to embrace *el hermano de JFK*; they seemed to be cut from the same bolt of revolutionary cloth.

The following day, 11/24/65, the Senator and his companions traveled further down the coast to Bahia, Brazil's 4th largest city — a former 16th-18th century Portuguese colony named San Salvador whose vast Black modern day population mirrors Portugal's centuries of enslaving Africans to make sugar. RFK toured the D'Alvas Matos Foundation's orphanage, where in his remarks, he ardently beseeched essential human guarantees, "Every child an education, every family adequate housing." His friends on the trip felt an urgency coming from him. The trip was almost over and, he felt, there was so much more to say and do.

Back in Rio for a November 25th speech at the Catholic University he aggressively implored the packed, student-filled auditorium to join the social reform movement sweeping Latin America.

From the 26th-29th the Senator's official travel log lists nothing. At that point, the Senator's fact-finding trip to South America was over — speeches delivered, questions engaged, press clippings generated.

Richard Goodwin now took over the itinerary and they all flew in a Varig charter to Manaus, largest port on the Amazon River. Leaving Ethel and most everyone else aboard a rustic paddlewheel the S.S. Percival Farquhar, RFK and Goodwin flew off in an antiquated 1930s seaplane. They took a side trip to the Nhamundú River, a meandering tributary of the Amazon River, where they played out their macho men's game of swimming with the piraña.

After leaving the Amazon, Goodwin insisted they stop in Caracas, Venezuela, thereby punctuating their three-week South American assessment with a Caribbean pit stop — addressing a convention of Latin American union leaders. Senator Kennedy's speech was a bold exclamation mark to their trip, "Last Chance for Democracy."

Now, seven months later, on our last night in Rio before heading north on Pan Am, we decided to embrace the national pastime and go dancing. The warm night air and raucous Brazilian rhythms were liberating.

At a dance club we heard a new song, *"Mais Que Nada"* played by Sergio Mendes and his group Brasil '66. Immediately, we bought the album. Wherever we went people were dancing the bossa nova. We danced along the Rio oceanfront till dawn. No one knew we had been in the Peace Corps. We blended in, shakin' our hips, rollin' our shoulders, bendin' our knees. Dance seemed to open one up.

Thrilled with our melodic musical discovery, so different from the screeching Andean *huaynos* (Indigenous folk dances), we flew north to Brasilia, the new capital that had been built in the middle of the country's vast wastelands to relieve the population pressures of Brazil's coastline living. Ninety-five percent of Brazil's 83 million citizens lived within 100 miles of the coastline, giving almost everyone a view of the ocean. (In 2020, Brazil had 211 million citizens.)

Brazil is a gigantic country, comprising more than half of the South American continent, giving the nation long gorgeous coastlines. Yet most of the interior is undeveloped Amazon basin, from the rain forests of Venezuela down to the outskirts of São Paulo, from Bahia on the Atlantic coast west to the impenetrable mato grosso and the soaring Andes.

One way to utilize this vast empty space was to move the capital out of congested Rio inland, and thereby force the leaders to move off the coastline.

In a huge, treeless, unpopulated savanna 1,200 miles south of the Amazon River, Brasilia, a totally modern urban complex, was built during the late 1950s and finally inaugurated in 1961.

The airplane-shaped city designed by famed Brazilian architect Oscar Niemeyer had no intersections, no stop signs. It was the ultimate planned modern city with prescribed neighborhood living: there was a church every two blocks of residential neighborhoods; every four blocks there was a school; every six blocks a shopping center.

When we arrived in Brasilia it was a Saturday, and this modern city was empty. The legislators flee the capital on Thursday evening and fly back to Rio, not returning until Monday morning. We rented a room at the American Consulate for $1.25 a night. No people in sight. The empty modern city looked like a post-nuclear war scene from the movie *On the Beach*. (Today, Brasilia is the country's 3rd largest city and has been declared a UNESCO World Heritage example of modern urban planning.)

From Brasilia, we continued flying north. Crossing over the Amazon River at 30,000 feet gave us an unparalleled view of the enormous river. When it empties into the Atlantic the mouth of the river is 200 miles wide! From its high Mantaro Valley origins in Peru to its jungle beginnings in Iquitos, where a two mile-wide nexus of Andean rivers form the mighty Amazon River as it travels east on its 3,900-mile journey across the South American continent. The river is home to pink dolphins, treacherous piraña, and tuna-sized *paiche*. It's the aorta of the Amazon's heart.

We hopscotched through the Caribbean, which was unbearably hot.

In Barbados, an almost entirely Black nation, no one worked in the scorching afternoon sun. The Hilton Hotel was the only establishment that had steel drum music where locals did the limbo and tourists exuberantly sang Harry Belafonte's calypso classic "Day-O."

Marie's parents met us in the Territory of Puerto Rico, one of Spain's earliest New World possessions . . . a 1493 fort made of volcanic rock.

As Marie was their only child, Ted and Marie were front and center as soon as we were back on American controlled soil. At first, we were hesitant to accept their generosity, but we soon moved into their luxury hotel — breakfast in bed, then enjoying a warm water pool lathered in suntan lotion with a Mount Gay rum and pineapple juice in hand, and gazed mindlessly out to sea.

Before leaving the island, we bought 12 bottles of duty-free alcohol. We had some serious catching up to do.

11

A LIFETIME AT IBM CORPORATE?

Finally in mid-July we landed at JFK airport, and shortly thereafter arrived in Brooklyn at my mother's family home in Park Slope, half a block from Prospect Park and the Brooklyn Zoo.

At the beginning of the 20th century, Park Slope was a new, highly prized Irish-Catholic neighborhood a few blocks from Grand Army Plaza, and the new IRT subway stop. My grandmother and her rich sisters owned homes in Park Slope.

But having your address on Carroll Street was like saying you sprinkled shamrocks over your steel-cut oatmeal. As an Irish-Catholic, you could not be more proud. The street was named after Charles Carroll IV, the only Catholic to sign the Declaration of Independence. He was the last man to sign it, and he was the last of the original signers to die, 56 years later. A fervent Irish-Catholic, Carroll joined the Revolution for its religious freedoms, which the Colony of Maryland did not grant. Carroll, founder of the Baltimore & Ohio Railroad, died at 91, and was reputedly America's richest man.

As historically grand and architecturally beautiful as Carroll Street was, my grandmother's narrow, 30-foot wide, three-story brownstone was, in my mind, tiny. She lived beneath the front door stoop where the coal used to be stored; and her youngest daughter's family filled up the 2nd and 3rd floors. Grandmother's rooftop garden was a two-foot by four-foot flower box of zinnias and petunias. Being raised in the wide-open spaces out West made life on Carroll Street feel claustrophobic to me. The house did, however, have a clever 'dumb waiter' that delivered food from the basement kitchen on up.

At a port in New Jersey, we were to pick up a new 1966 Volkswagen Bug from Germany that we had ordered through a dealership while we were still in Peru, and drive cross-country to California.

Our plan was to stop along the way at various Peace Corps/ Peru training camps, where we would stroke our egos by preparing new PCVs for Peru, and earn gas money to continue our journey west. Peru was Peace Corps' biggest program in Latin America, the second largest program in the world, and consequently there were a number of training programs in operation.

Reading the Sunday *New York Times* employment ads and drinking spicy Bloody Mary's in Brooklyn eventually led to the practical question: who do you want to work for the rest of your life? Who gives you the best chance at achieving some sense of freedom? Despite Earth being a self-sufficient enterprise everyone was required to "work for a living."

We were tempted by a career opportunity with IBM corporate's Labor Relations division, who would move us from California to Armonk, New York, the company headquarters.

IBM was so big they would never be bought out.

There was security in sticking with one company.

When they sent me to Armonk for my final interview, I asked IBM's Corporate VP of Labor Relations if I could wear a blue dress shirt; and he told me that if I felt good wearing one, no problem. It was a test of mine to see how prejudiced they felt towards workers . . . they passed.

Visiting our Nation's free art galleries in D.C., IBM arranged for me to have a physical. A future at IBM Corporate looked promising.

Dashing across country to California, we stopped for speaking gigs at Peace Corps training camps in Syracuse, New York and at University of Missouri, Kansas City.

Marie's and my occupational futures were our foremost concern, especially after two years of living a rudimentary lifestyle of no running water or flush toilets, candles and kerosene lanterns for light, and a wimpy, two-burner kerosene stove for frying toasted cheese sandwiches. Our minds wandered back to the Andes, where meat was only sold three times a week. The Quechua-speaking Native Americans who populated the Andes raised *cuyes* (guinea pigs) for their meat, and, as hard as it was to fathom, Peru had 5,000 varieties of potatoes.

But then, there were a number of anomalies about ancient Peru that no one in modern America had any answers for. We searched for answers, but the secrets of the Andes were too perplexing.

On our first Peace Corps vacation mid-1965, we took a three-hour train trip from 11,200-foot-high Cusco that ran alongside the Urubamba River as it descended into the *la montaña* (the Amazon jungle side of the Andes) to visit the incredible Inca citadel of Machu Picchu, spectacularly built into a lush 7,972-foot-high mountaintop.

We even climbed up the stone staircase of Huayna Picchu, an 8,835-foot sheer mountain peak that towers almost 900 feet above the ancient ruins of Machu Picchu, and whose tip is 2,500 feet above the Urubamba River directly below.

Coming back down Huayna Picchu's narrow, Incan-foot-sized stone steps had been a frightening descent, so steep some big-footed PCVs cried in fear they might fall from Huayna Picchu to the Urubamba River below.

That was the night Marie and I, and D.J. Boyd and his sister Jan, who was visiting from Montana, slept in the Temple of the Virgins, gazing up through the roofless stone buildings at the constellations above. The Incas used astronomy to guide their society, designing their buildings so that key astronomical measurements were encoded into their carved granite architecture. When we looked up into the heavens, we saw nothing but twinkling lights. Peru was beyond us.

Far from being the primitive land that everyone thought it was, Peru had a complex and elegant culture that was destroyed almost 500 years before by Spanish soldiers seeking gold (supposedly finding 20,000 shiploads), and by Catholic priests saving souls (supposedly millions died of European diseases and religious bigotry).

One of Peru's anomalies: Nazca Lines. Pre-Columbian geoglyphs in southern Peru picturing animals and plants. Shown here is a hummingbird. *Live Science*

Still, we left Peru puzzled as to how so few conquered so many, who, it turns out, ran a pretty sophisticated society. The Inca Empire bookkeeping system of knotted colored strings — *khipus* — remains undecipherable to this day.

Enormous public works were left by the Incas, and especially by those who preceded them at sites such as Chan Chan, Nazca, Sipán, Chachapoya, Paracas. Some works, like the Nazca Lines, were so long you could only see them from the sky! How had these gigantic, smooth stone buildings, walls, bridges, cities been constructed without mortar, and with what tools? Pyramids as old as Giza? Their extraordinary engineering achievement the *Qhapaq Ñan* (Grand Inca Road), emanating from its center in Cusco, established a 24,000 mile network of stone-paved, llama-friendly three meter-wide highways that ran across the tops of the Andes from northern Ecuador to southern Chile.

The list of Peru's unknown accomplishments is long. Archaeological ruins abound. Pick your region — coastal, mountains, or jungle. Even today, many mysteries remain accessible to the everyday blue-collar adventurer.

My parents met us in Las Vegas at the family favorite, Stardust Hotel. When Berdoo's own popular Arrowhead Springs Hotel & Spa had permanently closed, and after slot machines in California were outlawed in 1948, Las Vegas became the entertainment destination for the people of Berdoo — all-you-could-eat buffet and the most provocative stage shows in America.

Sitting in a booth with my family, waiting for the new Lido de Paris extravaganza to start, a Santa Fe switchman from Berdoo I hadn't seen in seven years came up to our table. He wanted to buy me a drink to thank me for standing up for him and the other three Black switchmen the Santa Fe had hired in early 1960.

It was a stark reminder of how white Southerners, who had migrated to California during the Great Depression, were as racist as their seedy rural relatives. When faced with the opportunity to act honorably, following the court's order to integrate, these transplanted white Southerners instead pulled a typical Confederate protest. If a Black man was put on the crew, they'd refuse to work on account of "sickness," shutting down the job until his replacement arrived. It was a classic, pointless protest that revealed their true illness — undeveloped moral fiber — hence their nickname of "crackers."

Once we had returned to Berdoo, passed out our gifts, and showed our slides of South America, I drove to UCLA. I wanted to discuss IBM's Labor Relations career option with my former political science advisor Dr. Irv Bernstein, whose legendary "take home" tests raised the bar on the world of university testing, as well as on university teaching. Irv, an expert on government/business/union relations, had mentored my senior thesis that dismissed the railroad industry's charges of "feather-bedding" and defended why railroad firemen were needed, and not for shoveling coal.

Seated in his Haynes Hall office, the genial Professor Bernstein, wearing his customary horn-rim glasses, bow tie, herringbone sport jacket and gray slacks, greeted me warmly, "How about those Bruins?" who had, since we last spoke, won two NCAA National Basketball championships under Coach John Wooden.

Irv's brother, Harry, covered unions for the *Los Angeles Times*. The Bernstein Brothers were nationally recognized for their expertise on government's needed control over commerce. Their message in a nutshell was: Unfettered capitalism fueled greedy dispositions that led to monopolies and civil unrest.

Irv explained that IBM paid their workers the union rate, rates contractually won at a Union Shop, but IBM didn't allow unions.

It was always a learning experience with Irv. You left his office feeling a little unfulfilled, but you always left smiling, realizing how he was always teaching us to think on our own. If IBM's going to pay union rates, why not allow a Union Shop? Hard to believe the biggest company would act so small as to oppose workers basic collective bargaining rights.

Then at the last minute, Marie and I decided against a lifetime at IBM Corporate.

We chose instead to become cross-cultural trainers for an 11-week Peace Corps/Peru training program conducted by the University of Missouri, Kansas City. The training would start Labor Day weekend and take place at a site in rural western Missouri, an hour south of Kansas City, called Allendale-by-Jingo.

Autumn in rural Missouri was a colorful world all of its own. In the spirit of the times locals told us, "The Negroes in your training group were welcome so long as they weren't seen in town after sundown."

Training for the Rural CD Peru 1966-68 program was designed by University of Missouri sociologist Dr. Oscar "Ozzie" Eggers. During WWII he had been trained by the Army to read, write, and speak Chinese. At this point in his life he had become less enamored with language training and more focused on a social-psychological level of communication.

Training consisted of five hours a day of Spanish language instruction, grubby farming experiences, and community development practices, but Ozzie included intense interpersonal exploration groups, role-playing . . . sensitivity training.

Being isolated, we ground it out 16 hours-a-day, seven days a week. It was a grueling ordeal. Harvard grads pleaded; Yale grads cried; everyone was begging for help, for understanding. Peace Corps Trainees "cut" by program evaluators — "de-selected" for not being good enough for the Peace Corps — ended up as draft board bait.

Our only respite was after dinner in the cafeteria where Marie would play the piano, often improvising, for an hour or more, unwinding from our stressful time living in 18th century Peru. Her after-dinner musical aperitif was the only thing that had nothing to do with training and everything to do with living.

I returned to Peru in late November to assist in the placement of the newly trained Volunteers, half of whom were young married couples escaping the draft.

Peruvians everywhere chuckled that Californians had elected a B-movie actor as Governor. Living in rural out-of-the-way Missouri, working full bore, I had totally missed the California gubernatorial campaign.

Indeed, I was surprised, but I did not see, as the Peruvians did, the humor of electing the co-star of governor.

Back in Los Angeles, I accepted a position starting January 1, 1967 with UCLA's Extension Division as an educational planner of short courses and conferences for business people.

We found a large, 1920s Mission Revival duplex in Lower Westwood, south of where the Mormon's Angel Moroni towered above the landscape. As in Peru, we had a red tile roof, lived on the second floor, and had a balcon (balcony) for sunset libations.

Yes, we were back in Western Civilization eating filet mignon and drinking Rusty Nails. We had returned from our extended honeymoon — a two-year training program for becoming agents of peaceful social change.

Our spacious 1,400 sq. ft. hardwood-floor home was draped

in hand-made Peruvian mementos — alpaca blankets and rugs, sweaters 'n vests, an engraved black leather-topped table, hammered silver ashtrays, pre-Colombian artifacts, and a dark red and black scene painted on a burlap Food for Peace sack.

We also spoke Foreign Service Officer level Spanish.

Foreign languages had long been the bane of my quest for higher education. Beginning French at UC Riverside in Fall 1960, all eleven students in my class, not counting me, already spoke French fluently. This resulted in me never understanding what the class was talking about. I took an Incomplete. Then my two years of Italian at UCLA sunk me in my final semester with a D. This left me with a deficit in language credits for my BA.

Shortly after arriving in Peru, UCLA's Registrar informed me that I lacked one language credit.

But after one year in the Peace Corps speaking Spanish, combined with my high school Spanish language capabilities, I was finally able to rise to an adult-speaking level, and my language deficiency was conquered.

During the summer of '65 I had taken and passed the Foreign Service Spanish Language proficiency exam at the U.S. Embassy in Lima, which gave me that lone required language credit; hence my official graduation occurred not in June of '63, but in January of '66 while serving overseas in the Peace Corps. I'm sure I was UCLA's only railroad switchman to graduate with a Bachelors of Arts that semester as well.

Many of the Santa Fe trainmen I had worked with saw UCLA as a "Little Red School house in the hills of Westwood," which was code for their Southern California-bred fear of being associated with, "JewCLA, a state school where Black athletes are welcomed."

Since its late 18th century formation by the Spanish, the City of Los Angeles quickly became a minority controlled area where the small wealthy Anglo-Protestant community dominated the racial and religious minorities, Indigenous and foreign born. One of the ways to keep control over that swarthy majority was to produce White Anglo-Saxon Protestant (WASP) propaganda denigrating and demeaning the various minorities who in fact were the majority. Codify that deceit into law and you've got control, but maybe not order.

Southern California's WASP culture treated racial and religious minorities far differently than the way New York City, America's largest and wealthiest city, treated its minorities.

It was weird growing up in Berdoo. New York was not even included in our school curriculum. Nor were the Aztecs, Mayan, or Incan cultures. Asia was unthinkable; American born-Japanese (Nisei) were jailed just to remind everyone who was in charge. The WASP dominated school boards fed us lots of European history, filled with kings and queens, which interested absolutely no one growing up in the 1950s.

In our two years abroad, we had learned to be skeptical of our government's good intentions. We had even started to question the Western notion of Peru's backwardness, a country whose ancient cultural remains go back thousands of years.

There were so many artifacts in Peru that on the streets of Lima and other urban centers Indigenous women sold "grave dolls" made of pre-Incan fabric they had unearthed while looking in the sand for *guacos*, (ancient pre-Colombian pottery). These were sought by both tourists and foreign museums.

One PCV from our Cornell group, Ralph Laird, while digging his backyard latrine in Arequipa, Peru's second largest city, uncovered 27 ceramic pots. Everywhere there were cultural remains.

Most PCVs brought home pre-Colombian artifacts in part because Peru was too poor to collect, guard, let alone excavate these archaeological treasures.

Between 1911 and 1913 Machu Picchu's re-discoverer, American Hiram Bingham, took boatloads of artifacts home to Yale for safe keeping [*National Geographic* 4/13/1913].

So did we, but on a much smaller scale. In early 1973, we worried that America might fall into revolution, so we donated our 18th century paintings from Potosi; Chancay, Chimu, and

Nazca pre-Colonial pottery; a woven coca bag; and swatches of pre-Incan fabrics to UCLA's new Fowler Cultural Museum.

Our two-year honeymoon had also started us wondering about the press. The bogus *Time Magazine* story about Huancayo and the "invisible" military vehicles that only New York editors could see; deceitful Norman Gall actively engaging PCVs in the Huancayo office for over a year, pretending to be on-assignment, when, in fact, he was using the Peace Corps office and unwitting PCVs as his cover while gathering information he sold to the CIA.

Manzanares Miguel and I knew it didn't take a year to write a story for the *Saturday Evening Post*. Was he spying on us?

And what was one to make of *The Washington Post's* November 14, 1965 story about RFK being told about the IPC controversy by "Peace Corpsmen," which clearly wasn't true? He had already known about it from President Belaúnde on down. The new staircase RFK stood on in Compone led to the newly constructed school library room, and not to some stalled AID project. And what was the purpose of changing the date of his November 11th visit to Cusco and Compone to the 13th, the day he and his entourage left Peru?

Fortunately, Cusco's *El Sol* newspaper published pre-stories, news stories, photos, even fully translated speeches of Robert Kennedy's November 11th visit to the Sacred Valley of Cusco. He came to see rural-based Peace Corps Volunteers in action and to engage the university youth of Cusco.

While the Peace Corps was given credit, and that was partially true, the fact is that it was Bob Kennedy's presence in Peru that forced the hypocrisy of the IPC controversy to be made public.

Robert Kennedy was an activist, as were his savvy colleagues. They were well-endowed warriors, smart and fearless, in pursuit of world peace. Exposing LBJ's dastardly deeds was all in a day's work.

The most erudite of my UCLA political science professors had been Dr. Thomas Paul Jenkin, who taught political philosophy, my major. His lectures were magnificent oratory, pure genius.

He never used notes, never stammered, never uttered an, "ah," never. His lectures were brilliant expositions of logic, ethics, and history woven together. It was like receiving profound knowledge in the fewest, most poetically encompassing words imaginable. I sat enthralled at every lecture, mesmerized by his eloquence. No greater exposition of philosophy have I heard since my two Political Theory classes with Professor Jenkin, the philosophy king, who suddenly gave up the front lines of teaching at UCLA to become the Vice Chancellor at UC Riverside, a most remarkable man.

Professor Jenkin always said, "Read the original. Read Voltaire and Rousseau; read Emerson and Thoreau. But do not read interpretations. Read the original." Which meant to me, go to the event and judge for yourself what's happening and be wary of "interpretations."

I was waiting for my new job with UCLA to start, which I knew was not what I wanted — educating business people, but it was a doorway into the world of adult education, which didn't involve having to lie to earn a living or in the dead of night having to leap five-feet from the top of one moving metal boxcar to another.

Anxious to catch up on the 30 months of modern living I had missed, I decided to see for myself the uproar that young people on Sunset Boulevard were causing.

Youth were congregating around the music clubs along the non-incorporated areas of Sunset Boulevard (now the City of West Hollywood).

Buffalo Springfield, a house band at Whiskey A Go-Go since mid-1966, had tapped into the tone of the emerging counterculture movement. Their countrified music attracted youthful audiences that did not want to go home after the last song. Locals had complained about the late night noise, so the authorities passed a 10 p.m. curfew for anyone under 18. Los Angeles County Sheriffs were being called in to protect the elderly Crescent Heights' community and local businesses from the youthful invaders. This would be a good opportunity to personally attend an event and compare it with the following day's news coverage.

Ground zero of the mounting demonstration against the 10 pm curfew was Pandora's Box, a treasured Beatnik coffee house sitting on a traffic island where Crescent Heights Boulevard met Sunset; Schwab's renowned ice cream parlor was only two stores away.

The evening crowds, numbering in the thousands, spread out along those streets. It was an unseasonably warm night; a dry Santa Ana wind was blowing through the Southland. On hand were 300 sheriffs earning hazard pay on top of overtime. Sheriff's prisoner buses, parked at the curb, snaked down Crescent Heights Boulevard ready to be filled.

Then I saw the so-called villains, the subject of such intense public scrutiny — a dozen or more scrawny curfew-breaking teenagers, most of whom were of modest size; taken all together not even a busload. Everyone else was standing around Pandora's Box waiting for something to happen.

A short, elderly Jewish woman explained to me her reason for being on the streets, "It's hot; nothing good on television. This, here, is nothing, but better than television."

"Why?" I asked.

"With no script," she winked encouragingly, "it could get exciting."

It was much ado about nothing.

The public happily paid for the expensively enforced curfew, at least that's the impression the media gave the following days. The establishment's effort to shut down the rebelling youth culture was in full force. Dissent was rising; the only place in public it was permitted was in song.

During late November, singer/songwriter Stephen Stills attended many of the Pandora Box demonstrations. They were encapsulations of an emerging national protest against the war and the status quo. These early counterculture musicians were singing, albeit in a low-key manner, about a new tomorrow based upon ancient truths and natural law. They were also complaining about the state of our democracy.

"Watch out," Stephen Stills warned, "Battle lines are being drawn. Nobody is right if everyone is wrong."

Responding to the civil unrest of Sunset Boulevard, Stills and company answered the establishment's heavy-handedness on December 6, 1966, recording "For What It's Worth."

"Hey," he plaintively asked, "what's that sound? Everybody look at what's goin' down?"

The message was obvious to everyone but our leaders. Stills' song was an epiphany that bound the members of the counter-culture together, a prescient signal to all like-minded of what was to come.

My educational planning position with UCLA Extension was an academic appointment, which meant my Bachelor's degree made me the lowest of the low amongst UCLA's academicians. Chancellor Franklin Murphy had both an MD and a Law degree.

Still, as low as I was on the academic totem pole, I was able to buy faculty season tickets to Pauley Pavilion, and to personally cheer on Coach John Wooden's sensational NCAA Basketball Championship runs every spring. As a member of the revered KELPS, UCLA's legendary 'spirit' group, it was our lifetime duty to cheer on the Bruins, especially at away games, a tradition started by Coach Wooden when he first came to UCLA in 1948.

KELPS had been founded the year before by fun-loving WWII veterans returning to campus on the GI Bill. After being voted in — unanimously — KELPS members were issued a unique blue and gold 1930s-style cabbie's cap.

In December 1954, they followed Wooden cross-country in an old school bus all the way to Madison Square Garden. They strutted into the Garden wearing their KELP hats and UCLA letterman sweaters, and started throwing Sunkist oranges to the crowd. The spirited KELPS softened the tough veneer of New Yorkers and made headlines in the new *Sports Illustrated Magazine* (January 1955).

The reason for the KELPS popularity on campus is that they were UCLA's first multi-racial, multi-cultural men's group.

U.C.@L.A. was established in 1919 — U.C. Berkeley's Southern Campus. The post-WWII KELPS were the ultimate expression of California's public higher education goals — the University of California was for everyone. Belonging to the prankster-playing KELPS was the most desired male student association on campus for 23 years (1947-1970).

Truth be told . . . a close reading of UCLA's annual student publication *Southern Campus: 1947–1948* reveals that a kindly group of female students, The Trolls, pulled off a photo prank that gave birth to UCLA's manly KELPS.

Playing pranks had been high performance art during the 1950s. By the Sixties, prank playing and public protests had merged, but the fact that the war never ended took the fun out of prank playing; nothing about war and riots was funny.

The last person whose photograph appeared in a Southern Campus annual wearing a KELP hat was the much admired film actress Raquel Welch in 1970. Fun finally lost out at UCLA; students were now deadly serious, fighting the prospect of being a warrior for a bad cause.

Sitting in my faculty seats at Pauley Pavilion — watching Coach Wooden perform his magic — was a classic Sixties experience where the public school team beat the pants off the rich establishment schools, season after season. Three of Wooden's early greats were KELPS: two were black and one was white, whose name was Green. We public school unknowns took heart watching Wooden's fast-breaking guards conduct full court presses every play of the game. It was an historic moment. Basketball was being fundamentally changed, along with everything else. Change in play, change in players. Change was everywhere in everything.

Working at UCLA had also meant exposure to its many cultural amenities, my favorite being the Distinguished Speakers who were brought to campus and paid top dollar to speak their piece and to field questions. Big colleges had student fees from many students, which enabled them to pay top dollar to the top newsmakers of the day. The best part was the Question & Answer period that followed. Gave you a chance to talk truth to power.

In November 1961 U.S. Senator Barry Goldwater of Arizona (R) was scheduled to speak at Royce Hall, one of UCLA's original four buildings. His subject: Fidel Castro and the Cuban Revolution that had claimed victory on January 1, 1959, and chased Cuba's despicable dictator Fulgencio Batista into exile. The Cuban Revolution had many American admirers, but the Eisenhower Administration saw Castro as an impediment to continuing their economic hegemony over Latin America.

Anxious to gain U.S. support for the Cuban Revolution and its desire to diversify its sugar-based economy, Castro visited New York City on April 15, 1959, and he came again on September 18, 1960 to speak at the UN. On both occasions, the Eisenhower government snubbed him.

According to veteran reporter Don Fulsom's deeply researched books — *Nixon's Darkest Secrets* and *The Mafia's President* — by early 1960 Vice President Nixon had formed the anti-Castro CIA group Operation 40, and had green-lighted contracts with the Mafia to eliminate Castro. He failed, though, to launch the invasion of Cuba before the Kennedy Administration took over.

Given the Bay of Pigs fiasco in April 1961, there was no bigger political issue in the Western Hemisphere than Fidel Castro and the Cuban Revolution. After two years of failing to establish a relationship with Washington, Castro, on July 26,1961, announced Cuba's allegiance to the Soviet Union that promised the Cuban Revolution financial support.

Some hoped Kennedy's election would lead the U.S. to productively engage emerging nations instead of sending them into the enemy camp. However, how to deal with Castro was a classic hawks-vs.-doves argument . . . use a club or offer love.

I had taken a class on Latin American politics to learn how experts deal with Latin American wars of liberation, whether by

breaking from colonists or from dictators. But UCLA's esteemed
Latin American Affairs Professor Russell Fitzgibbon refused to
discuss Castro . . . "It was outside the course outline." We would
not be studying revolution, instead we would be studying "cau-
dillos," whatever that meant.

It was anticipated that the November appearance on campus of
conservative U.S. Senator Barry Goldwater would be a red meat
affair — political theater at its best — staged in UCLA's most
glorious building. What would Goldwater say? What would be
his philosophical rationale for overthrowing Castro?

At the time, I was working midnights to 8 a.m. in downtown
LA at Union Station, moving passenger trains to and from the
washers, as crews cleaned them inside and out for their next run.

When I got off work the day of the Goldwater lecture, all I
had to do was drive up Alameda Street to Philippe's and take
Sunset Boulevard west all the way to campus — the only street
in LA that goes directly to UCLA. Since I was living in Santa
Monica, 6 miles west of campus, I didn't bother to go home to
change, and wore my blue denim railroad clothes to the speech.
I didn't want to miss any of this historic face-off between a cow-
boy conservative and UCLA's liberal student body.

As it was, I was lucky to get a seat in the upper balcony as
Royce Hall was packed. The elegant 1,900-seat theater was
noisier than a train station at rush hour.

Goldwater, a department store heir, began his talk blustering
that Cuba's revolution wasn't anything compared to ours.

He went on for 20 minutes, taunting the audience with his
"we should Invade Cuba" diatribe. Next he took questions for
another 30. Finally, he announced, "One more question."

Out of the dozens of arms wildly signaling a question, the
Senator chose me, sitting high up in the balcony, 200 feet from
the stage where he couldn't see my soot-covered work clothes.

I shouted my upper-balcony question/statement that took
Goldwater to task for his failure to acknowledge, "Cuba's sover-

eignty, dismissing its right of self-determination."

Goldwater responded by invoking the 19th century Gunboat Diplomacy standard, "We can just liberate Cuba."

His bullying rhetoric produced an immediate outrage that shook even the chandeliers. The *Daily Bruin* editorial staff led by Harry Shearer, in their November 14, 1961 issue, declared Senator Goldwater, "might yet be the voice of folly."

Point in fact, Goldwater lost the 1964 Presidential election to LBJ in a landslide, winning just five Southern states and Arizona, and only 39% of the popular vote.

Not all questions from the floor generate such a response. Sometimes the answer is personal and you discuss the answer with yourself. Privately.

That's what happened to me later when I heard Stanford University's new Student Body President and founder of the anti-draft organization, The Resistance, David Harris speak at Meyerhoff Park in 1967.

He was a most provocative speaker, and one who upset my military way of thinking the most. He had a lot to say about being a Conscientious Objector to war. "I will not play the game," he adamantly declared, a position he fervently advocated that ultimately sent him to Federal prison from 1969 to 1971.

What stuck with me was his assertion that "warriors had no right to kill another man's son or daughter." Does the state have the right to order a man to kill another man's child? Are we God's children or not? If we are, I can't imagine any higher being seeing the murder of God's children very favorably. "Thou Shalt Not Kill" doesn't have much wiggle room.

I was not the only one attracted to Harris' courageous anti-war arguments. Popular folk singer and vocal anti-Vietnam War protester Joan Baez married Harris before year's end.

Even high-profile couples were coming out against war. Mainly, though, young women were in the front lines of the anti-war protests and concerts I went to. Most of the young men stood at the back protecting their rears.

12

WAR & PEACE

By the end of 1966, LBJ's Vietnam War had become a monstrous military undertaking, as well as an ethical nightmare. Money and men were being poured into Vietnam to no good effect — rising from 16,300 advisors in December 1963 to 185,000 combat troops by the end of 1965 to 385,000 troops by December of 1966!

In January 1967 U.S. Congress approved the federal budget, which contained $2 billion in domestic spending and $22 billion to finance the Vietnam War! Anti-War protests were as much about saving lives as about saving America's gold-backed treasury. Every year cost us dearly, not to mention the defenseless Vietnamese peasants we incessantly sprayed with Monsanto's toxic Agent Orange, and bombed mercilessly with DOW Chemical Company made napalm. Scientific barbarism was rising to new heights.

Besides escalating the Vietnam War in early 1967, LBJ began pushing his domestic War on Poverty. On the point, he had the charismatic Sargent Shriver; and at the grass roots, millions of dollars were being distributed to community action agencies, so long as local politicians approved.

In almost direct programmatic opposition, RFK officially started his version of fighting urban poverty by establishing in the heart of Brooklyn the nation's first urban community development corporation: The Bedford Stuyvesant Restoration Corporation. Surrounded by activists and bankers, RFK sounded his charge: "We start from this truth, if there is to be a revitalization of Bedford Stuyvesant and places like it, methods must be found to join human resources with capital resources. No society ever thrives without this marriage."

His seat on the Senate Sub-Committee: Employment, Manpower and Poverty afforded Kennedy even deeper involvement in resolving issues of poverty.

Hearings were held March 13 through 17 in D.C. where Marian Wright, a young ACLU civil rights attorney from Mississippi, beseeched committee members to visit the impoverished Delta, as she described the woeful poverty and malnutrition devastating sharecroppers' unemployed by recent crop mechanizations.

Accepting her challenge, Chairman Joseph P. Clark of Pennsylvania and Senator Robert F. Kennedy scheduled hearings in Jackson, Mississippi for April 9 and 10 and the results proved startling. Conditions were even worse than imagined. The American public was shocked to learn of such widespread malnutrition in the wealthiest country on Earth. Quickly, the issues of poverty and malnutrition became page-one news.

In the spring, so called, "Negro" leaders began breaking ranks with those in support of the Vietnam War. Dr. Martin Luther King Jr. on the 4th of April gave his famous Anti-War speech: "Beyond Vietnam: A Time to Break Silence," in which he said, "A Nation that continues to spend more money on military defense than on programs of social uplift is approaching spiritual death."

World Heavyweight Champion Muhammad Ali argued to his Draft Board that he had "No quarrel with the Vietcong," and on April 28th declared himself, "a Conscientious Objector in opposition to the War in Vietnam." In breaking with the political establishment these "Negro" leaders suddenly became Black leaders.

In May, local peace activist Irving Sarnoff organized Los Angeles' first Anti-Vietnam War March for June 23rd and chose as its leaders: Muhammad Ali and Dr. Benjamin Spock, author of multi-million seller *Baby and Child Care* and co-director of National Committee for Sane Nuclear Energy (SANE). Courageously the two activists led an Anti-Vietnam War protest march from neighboring Rancho Park into Los Angeles' sophisticated Century City.

Los Angeles' first Anti-Vietnam War March of 10,000 was genuinely peaceful and surprisingly white — white-coated doctors and nurses, white-collar workers, and thousands of white college students from Westside campuses.

Century City Anti-Vietnam War March — 6/23/1967
L-R: Sharon Goodner, Jay Gotfredson, Sweet William, Marie Evensen, D.J. Boyd. *Photo by Sweet William. Published by LA Free Press: "Asian War is Coming Home" 6/25/67*

Waiting for them were 1,300 LAPD police officers armed to the teeth. Like modern day Centurions, they surrounded Century City's new crown jewel — the Century Plaza Hotel, where MCA movie mogul Lew Wasserman was hosting a $500-a-plate fundraiser for LBJ's 1968 Presidential Re-Election Campaign.

Across the street from the Century Plaza Hotel, while marching back and forth on the sidewalk with our posters held high, I ran into Phil Friedman, a UCLA cohort from 1963 whom I had helped run ASUCLA's Distinguished Speakers Program.

Phil had been elected by the student body, and I, a volunteer, had had the honor of eating an expensive dinner together one night at Trader Vic's in Beverly Hills with the author John Dos Passos who had just flown in from Brazil to give a "$3,000-plus-hotel" speech to the student body.

Phil said he was now working for IBM. I told him of almost joining IBM and how the corporate VP of Labor Relations told blue-collar me that I could "wear a blue dress shirt if I felt it looked good."

Friedman laughed. "Sure, but don't expect to be promoted. Someone who doesn't understand the value of Tom Watson's white-shirt edict just doesn't move ahead." He jabbed me in the ribs and winked, "Not all labor relations specialists are meant to be managers; it's a very bossy job."

Back and forth we marched all afternoon.

It was my Dad's 49th birthday, and we had to split for Berdoo. We had said we'd be there late for dessert. We parked The Bug on Century Park West for a fast get-a-way.

Not five minutes after leaving Century City, the KHJ radio broadcaster covering the March, suddenly started screaming. Late in the day, as LBJ and his cronies watched the parading protesters from the safety of the Century Plaza Hotel balconies, the heavily armed LAPD suddenly, and without provocation, attacked and violently beat thousands of unarmed white protesters.

LBJ and his cadre of hawks had upped the ante on backing the war until he couldn't travel anywhere in America without hearing the chant: "Hey, Hey, LBJ, how many kids did you kill today? Hey, Hey, LBJ . . .."

Similarly, the outrageous Broadway musical *HAIR* turned that anti-establishmentarian sentiment into a sorrowful soliloquy of acronyms that revealed who was at fault for the Vietnam War, "LBJ . . . FBI, CIA . . . LSD." Creators Jerome Ragni and Gerald Rado opened *HAIR* in every major city around the world, spreading seeds of an emerging counterculture — its ethos, its diversity, its high-steppin' path to happiness.

The Beatles avant-garde album cover for *Sgt. Pepper's Lonely Hearts Club Band* aligned the lads with America's cultural greats. Musically, they offered the rock 'n roll alternative of everyday peace and love to a society long obsessed with war and violence. "With a Little Help From My Friends" became a venerated song of the grass-rooted movement. A serotonin-producing flower bud was its frontline weapon.

The President had become hostage to his own ill-conceived war plans. His June 23rd fundraising stop in Century City was the last time LBJ appeared in public as President. From that protest on, LBJ only appeared at military bases. The tide of dissent was rapidly rising.

The facts were obvious: America and all of its technological superiority were conducting a heinous over-the-top war against a Third World rice-fed opponent. Yet this bullying effort was being openly rejected by millions of Americans, even heroic veterans did the unthinkable and publicly returned to the Department of Defense their medals of valor.

More importantly, the government's bad behavior was being replaced with progressive ideas, social experimentation, and age-old utopian beliefs. The Sixties, in spirit and in action, was a major break from the status quo.

The counterculture movement swiftly became, amongst the young, the new normal. Electrified music and the natural world of serotonin-producing substances facilitated the difficult, but necessary task of psychologically breaking away from the mainstream culture and its moral and ethical hypocrisies. The changes the Nation was going through were gut wrenching, morally realigning, and physically demanding. We were transitioning ourselves from war to peace, from booze to pot, from bras to not.

It was an age-old search: what is our natural state in this world of contentious political and ethical beliefs? Everything in

America had a price and something for nothing was considered without value. It turns out, hugs, kisses, backrubs — absolutely priceless items — were undercutting capitalism's profit ethos.

Confusion ruled. One side hated the other for not wanting to kill unknown brown-skinned people halfway around the world, even when no one could see what they were doing. Instead, the other side signaled, No Contest, and declared, "We're outta here." And without a fight, these Americans quietly began disappearing into the rural countryside, giving birth to the Back to the Land movement.

Change was instant. GI Joe buzz cuts suddenly were passé; long hair ruled. Beards flowed, bras burned. Mr. and Ms. Natural were in vogue; processed food was not. Artifice was out. Makeup and hairspray were discarded. The quest to be natural was widespread.

America's deceitful political leadership and our military's egregious misuse of power — famously characterized by Robert Kennedy as, "Swatting mosquitoes with a sledge hammer" — produced an army of millions of anti-establishment supporters who were intent on overthrowing the status quo. These supporters were not only against the Vietnam War; they were for cultural and economic improvements and, not surprisingly, for justice. The counterculture was rural and urban, elite and working class, racially and religiously diverse.

All this movement lacked was a leader.

Senator Robert Kennedy knew if he opposed LBJ the establishment would call their conflict personal and they would continue to ignore the war raging out of control 10,000 miles from home. The American-led War in Vietnam, from its napalm bombing of grass shack villages to its spraying of DNA-damaging pesticides on local agriculture, was morally reprehensible and ultimately proved to be economically disastrous for the United States, except for those companies in the business of war. There was no hiding from the debacle. TV's nightly news coverage was broadcast to a stunned nation being told that for patriotic reasons they had to fight peasants in Southeast Asia or we'd lose an all-important game of international dominos. Do not question authority was their blunt message. Dissent was demonized, even considered un-American. Pressure on Senator Kennedy not to fracture the Democratic Party kept him in check, although anti-war activists kept pressing him to oppose LBJ and his metastasizing war.

There were so many casualties the Department of Defense term "Killed-in-Action," an all-important marker for the public, was replaced with an acronym KIA. Media experts reported that too much "killing" in the news was depressing viewers, especially the families of lost soldiers. There was a growing lament in the land over the grandchildren not being born, over the fatherless daughters, the wayward sons, rioting in the streets, black men being shot in their sleep.

The culture of killing was a demon burrowed deep in the American body politic. America, as a Nation, began with a war. We've saved the world winning wars. The atomic bombing of Hiroshima and Nagasaki proved we were the unquestionable masters of murder, killing young and old, rich and poor, good and bad, all in one fell swoop. Even our citizenry was heavily armed for violent war should peace breakout.

Personally, I was incensed by the Los Angeles establishment's vilification of peaceful First Amendment-protected protesters. Jaundiced media coverage of the LAPD's Century City riot condoned wanton violence by LAPD officers against unarmed citizens. Even worse, the LAPD justified their criminal behavior in that they were operating under the preposterous pretense that the unarmed, white protesters posed, "A National Security threat to those inside the Century Plaza Hotel." No doubt an impediment to fundraising.

It was no secret. The establishment wanted to punish protesters without any due process and thereby discourage other citizens from protesting. At first Los Angeles' mass media turned a blind eye to the violence. Then later, according to a former President of Los Angeles Police Commission, they didn't.

Los Angeles Times reporters complained in-house about how the paper miss-characterized the police riot, a fact that was eventually acknowledged by the publisher. Supposedly, it was a *Los Angeles Times* first to not stand with the police.

Our contingent of five well-dressed protesters was photographed numerous times, mostly by a team of Hispanic men wearing dark suits and black fedoras that few in Los Angeles ever wore. Our photo of clean-shaven, short-haired protesters appeared in the *LA Free Press'* June 25th 'Post-Police Riot' EXTRA, while the *Los Angeles Times* in their coverage published photos of bloodied, bearded long-haired protesters. Each paper had its protester image already in mind. In our coats and ties, we were too straight looking for the mainstream media and just perfect for the alternative press.

The news that everyone published in brutal detail was the rising number of destructive civil disturbances, urban and suburban. City after city was being struck by marauding swarms of angry Black protesters frustrated with society's refusal to end racism and to stop blatant segregation.

In July, major cities suffered catastrophic losses — Newark and Detroit — prominent black communities went up in smoke; ghetto landlords lost their properties, residents lost their homes; National Guard troops were mobilized. President Johnson was beside himself; he had war at home and abroad. America was as charred as Vietnam. As a stopgap measure, the President on July 28th formed a National Advisory Commission on Civil Disorders, chaired by former Illinois Governor Otto Kerner, to explore what was behind these devastating riots. During the first nine months of 1967 there were 164 civil disturbances. The Commission picked 75 of them to study in depth. A report was due in early 1968.

The Nation — black and white, rich and poor — was in deep despair.

13

THE SHOESHINE BOY

Once Frank Mankiewicz had taken over Senator Kennedy's press office in May of '66, his network of social change activists from his years in the Peace Corps soon followed — making contacts and building alliances. Change was in the air. Mankiewicz's view that the Peace Corps was "A Revolutionary Force" appealed to many PCVs who had served in Latin America. Mank, an experienced social change activist, was our spokesman.

Mankiewicz's career with the Peace Corps had begun, back in August 1961, inside an El Paso motel room. Mank found himself surrounded by Sargent Shriver and his pals William Haddad, a JFK aide who became the Peace Corps' first Inspector General (1961-63) and Fletcher Knebel, author of the first Peace Corps novel *The Zin-Zin Road* (1966).

They cajoled, they pleaded, are you on board? Finally, Frank folded to their pressure and agreed to become Peace Corps country director in Peru. According to Coates Redmond in her entertaining account of the Peace Corps' earliest days, *Come As You Are*, Shriver cackled in happiness.

In September, Mankiewicz accompanied Sargent Shriver on his first tour of South America to identify prospective field offices and to discuss various social change strategies. Peru was to be the Peace Corps' first Latin American country, and Frank, a seasoned activist, was ready to roll.

Early on, Mankiewicz had hired Ralph C. Guzmán to be his regional representative for Chimbote, a lowbrow fishing port on the arid north coast of Peru where it sometimes doesn't rain for a century.

Like Mankiewicz, Guzmán was a WWII veteran. Unlike Frank, a scion of Beverly Hills, Guzman was a Mexican immigrant of the 1930s who grew up in East Los Angeles during the Great Depression. Frank grew up on the west side of L.A., son of famed *Citizen Kane* screenwriter Herman Mankiewicz. While Frank went to UCLA and Columbia for an MA in Journalism, Ralph used his G.I. Bill in the 1950s to earn a B.A. and an M.A. from L.A. State College (now Cal State L.A.). He was UCLA's first doctoral candidate to explore the Chicano Movement.

By the time he met Mankiewicz, Guzmán was already a veteran activist who had been involved in the formation of the legendary Community Service Organization (CSO) in East L.A., a post-WWII effort to identify and activate the growing Mexican American community.

It was a joint Mexican-Jewish venture largely financed by the Los Angeles Jewish community that had deep roots in the East L.A. neighborhood of Boyle Heights. At the beginning of the 20th century Los Angeles Jews were severely limited by where they could live, what professions they could enter, and the business associations they could join. During the Great Depression Mexican immigrants arrived in increasing numbers causing cultural friction. The Zoot Suit riots during WWII raised the fear that violence would follow the war, which led L.A. Jews to believe their security was tied to the plight of their impoverished Mexican American neighbors.

In 1947, CSO was incorporated by Edward Roybal, Antonio Rios, and Fred Ross Sr., the legendary community organizer and associate of Saul Alinsky from Chicago's Industrial Areas Foundation. They began by registering voters every step of the way; eventually in 1949 they elected WWII vet Ed Roybal to the Los Angeles City Council, and later in 1962 to U.S. Congress, making him California's 1st Spanish-surnamed congressman since 1879. Fred Ross was an inspirational organizer who opened CSO chapters throughout California.

In San Jose, he trained a young César Chávez, and later in Stockton he taught 25 year-old Dolores Huerta, his in-home organizing techniques. It wasn't long before César and Dolores took CSO organizing to the next level.

In 1962 they left CSO to start a union for farmworkers.

When Dolores and Fred Ross asked Alinsky for help, he told them, "The farmworkers are a lost cause."

Alinsky was a coalition man, and wanted to bring all the organizations together to create a power base, whereas Fred and his disciples were home oriented, working with penniless activists, not with organizations.

Meanwhile in East L.A., Guzmán was busy legitimizing their efforts; he filed CSO's first federal tax exemption and started their first newspaper, the *CSO Reporter*, and became its first editor-in-chief. He was a news reporter working throughout East L.A., and an assistant editor for the *LA Daily News*. And when Guzmán heard JFK's call to join the New Frontier, Mankiewicz was the beneficiary.

PCV Catherine DeLorey (Univ. Denver CD 1963-1965) remembered Guzmán, his wife Stella, and their children:

> RALPH WAS highly respectful of our client, the citizens of Chimbote; he was totally committed to improving the public health system of Chimbote, center of Peru's pungent anchovy fishmeal industry. Ralph was thrilled that my roommate and I were public health nurses.

PCVs said you could smell the coastline community of Chimbote from 30 kilometers (18 miles) away. Chimbote, a small, sleepy 19th century fishing village, had ridden the 35-year boom and bust of the lucrative *guano* (bird excrement) fertilizer industry: 1845–1880.

The Humboldt Current (aka the Peru Current) brings a 500 mile-wide swath of cold water north toward the Equator. The rapidly moving current contains billions of tiny fish that attract millions of birds, who found the rocky, barren Chincha Islands of Chimbote Bay a perfect place to poop. Ground zero for these seabirds was the volcanic island, *Isla Blanca* (White Island), covered white in bird excrement.

We're talking mountains 150 feet tall of fowl-smelling guano collected over millennia. Spanish conquerors, of course, did
nothing with the windfall, but 19th century British industrial-
ists looking to extract Peru's mineral wealth were armed with
chemists who soon realized Chinchas' organic guano was the
world's best fertilizer. Eventually, 12 million tons were shipped
to Europe, Australia, and the southern United States. Guano
wealth went into the private pockets of Lima entrepreneurs until
the beginning of the 1870s when Peru's leaders began financing
Henry Meiggs' railroad building enterprises with guano profits.

As the 1960s began, so began the creation in Chimbote of
the anchovy-based fishmeal industry (farm animal food) that in
one decade grew to 100 fishmeal manufacturing plants, making
Peru the world's top fishery! In the first four years, its population went from 4,000 residents to a bustling town of 40,000. By
1969, of Chimbote's 177,000 residents, 93% had migrated from
the Andes. Indigenous families had escaped en masse the cruel
rigors of Andean living, a life absent of health and educational
resources, and completely void of opportunity. Shunned by the
caudillo-led *mestizo* class, *serranos* were on their own, members
of a long ago defeated empire.

The booming anchovy fishmeal industry, plus the development of a steel plant, had triggered an avalanche of Andean
peasants from the Ancash region. They were seeking a new life
at the coast. Chimbote's pungency was legendary; its malodor-
ous menu of the 1960s ... *anchovy al fresco*.

Quite unexpectedly, in one of the dusty shantytowns of
Chimbote, a surprising validation of the Peace Corps' daring
community development strategy occurred. PCVs siding with
the poor, as Mankiewicz had directed, living with them in their
makeshift communities resulted in a storybook outcome. It was,
in a nutshell, what JFK envisioned the Peace Corps would ac-
complish — to embolden peasants to become presidents.

There was complete agreement amongst PCVs in Peru that
the unstructured community development approach to social
justice and economic improvement was difficult, rife with the

failures and frustration of crossing cultures. It was hard to discern if the whole effort was even worth it. We were trying in two years to right wrongs that had been in play for centuries. Nevertheless, the Peace Corps in Chimbote, by doing the most basic of human acts, overturned centuries of harsh discrimination. At the time, it was hard to believe their simple outreach would have long-lasting implications for millions of Indigenous Native Americans. But it did.

When PCVs Nancy Deeds and Joel Meister (Wisconsin CD 1963-1965) arrived in Chimbote, it was considered a "hard duty" assignment. Regional Director Ralph Guzmán assigned them to live in one of Chimbote's many shantytowns. Going door-to-door, seeking a space for Nancy to call her own, the third house Nancy and Joel visited was that of Anatolio and Margarita Toledo, who had migrated in 1959 from the mountains of Ancash, along with their 9 surviving children. Part of what sent the Toledos in search of a new world was that 7 of their 16 children had died by the age of five. In the Andes, there were no medical resources, no education; all they had was a small plot of land that had been tilled for centuries.

Margarita Toledo told Nancy she had no room to rent. There was, however, a space in the front room with a small window from which she sold minor items like chewing gum and matches. Her street-savvy 16-year-old son, Alejandro, did the math and calculated that the rent Nancy would pay per month far exceeded his Mom's monthly window sales.

After Nancy moved into the small space, Alejandro helped Joel find a place to live, ultimately scoring an abandoned animal stall that Joel cleverly converted into a living space. For Alejandro, these blonde-haired blue-eyed gringos were an unexpected opportunity that literally knocked on his front door. These hijos de JFK happily addressed his questions that no one else had answers for. Nancy, a Cornell graduate, Joel, a Stanford graduate, became his mentors.

Even more intriguing to young Alejandro was the Peace Corps' regional director, Ralph Guzmán, a Mexican American intensely interested in helping Chimbote and in understanding who Peru's Native Americans were. "He was an extraordinary man," Alejandro remembered, "very smart, and very kind. Several times we went down to the harbor to eat *cerviche* and to talk. He was an intellectual, but not at all pretentious."

As a 4 1/2 year-old, Alejandro had been a *lustrador de zapatos* (shoeshine boy); in Chimbote, as a 14 year-old student, he sold tamales at night down by the harbor. He already knew higher education for Andean people was not in the cards.

Being from Chimbote was another strike against his ambition for higher education. Everyone in Lima knew Chimbote, even though it was a coastal community, was filled with Andean immigrants.

His father, a mason, had begun a new trade and began to mine the sea.

Alejandro later explained:

EVERYTHING THAT lived in the sea we ate. But if you want to know, it was eating all that seafood, eating every creature imaginable, that gave me lots of Omega-3, lots and lots of Omega-3. That's what oiled my intellectual motor, that's what fueled my hunger for knowledge.

Talking with PCVs, Alejandro learned that in America he, an Indigenous person, would have the opportunity to obtain a higher education that caudillo authorities in Peru wouldn't let him pursue.

Like elsewhere in Peru, all this PCV peacemaking led to love. Nancy and Joel decided to marry. Their parents, though, couldn't come to Peru, so Guzmán offered the Peace Corps regional office for the marriage ceremony. Alejandro's parents stepped forward to be the *Padrino* and the *Madrina* (godfather and godmother) of their wedding, an important obligation in Peruvian society. March 1, 1965 Chimbote's Peace Corps office celebrated Peru's first in-country marriage of PCVs. Nancy recalled the day,

How FORTUNATE we were to have Ralph as our Regional Rep. He had that Latin cultural sensibility and spoke Spanish fluently. With none of our family present, Ralph and Stella being very supportive of us getting married saved the day.

Teen-aged Alejandro was surprised at how interested Guzmán was in cultural identity. "He's the first person I ever heard use the word 'Chicano,' Alejandro recalled. "I asked him what it meant, and he said it was a name for 'people from Mexico who had immigrated to the United States.'"

In 1965 Nancy and Joel took Alejandro on his first trip to Lima, 250 miles down the Pan American Highway, where he met Mankiewicz, who greeted him with his longshoreman growl, "I've heard about you."

"He spoke to me in English, I answered in some English," Alejandro was proud to say. PCV Marjorie Lam (San Diego State CD 1964-1966) had been giving him English lessons in exchange for Quechua lessons. Alejandro again asked questions and he got more of the same answers. There was no way Peruvian universities would accept him. He was Andean, and worse than that, he was a smelly Chimbotano. As Nancy and Joel's two-year obligation came to a close in late '65, they gave Alejandro their advice.

If YOU COME to San Francisco to get a higher education and you want us to sponsor you then you must promise us that you will return to Peru. We don't want to foster any brain drain. Also, get a student visa so you don't get drafted.

Nineteen-year-old Alejandro arrived in the Bay Area end of December 1965; and in a return of favors, the new arrival ended up sleeping on Nancy and Joel's couch. They were both enrolled in UC Berkeley graduate programs: social work and sociology, and happily helped Alejandro enter Jesuit-run University of San

Francisco (USF) that had an excellent language program. Overnight, Alejandro's world had been transformed, from the stark
and dusty Chimbote oceanfront to the green and fog-shrouded
hillsides of Berkeley, California. He reveled in the newness of
his world and in his newfound freedom. Soon, he began to engage in the swirling Bay Area scene of the mid-Sixties: hippies
of Haight-Ashbury, anti-war demonstrations marching down
Market Street, an emerging Black Panther movement in Oakland headed by Huey Newton and Eldridge Cleaver.

César Chávez's newly announced Delano Grape Strike
(1965-1970) and its support of migratory farmworkers capti-
vated Alejandro; so much attention in America given to what
were mostly penniless undocumented workers. Fascinated by
the growing momentum for Chávez's grape boycott, Alejandro
went to a protest in the Mission District that Chávez was leading. After hearing Chávez speak of "Chicanos," Alejandro introduced himself and told César he was a USF student from Peru.
When Chávez asked how he afforded a private college, Alejandro responded with a quick foot move, "soccer scholarship," he
proudly answered. He told Chávez that hearing him talk about
Chicanos reminded him of an American he met in Peru. "You
should meet Ralph Guzmán;" Alejandro urged César, "he's an
extremely smart Mexican American who, like you, speaks of a
growing Chicano movement."

Alejandro never forgot their twenty-minute conversation.
"We spoke in Spanish. Not really knowing where I lived in Peru,
Chávez asked me what was Guzmán doing in Peru; and when
I told him he was a staff person with the Peace Corps, he was
astonished."

You can imagine César's surprise of being told by a 21-year
old Native American from Peru to be on the lookout for an
emerging Chicano leader who had worked for JFK's Peace
Corps.

Following his graduation from USF with a BA degree in economics and business administration in 1970, Alejandro would
go on to win a scholarship to Stanford University, where he

would earn three advanced degrees: an MA in education, MA in economics, and a Ph.D in human resources from the graduate school of education.

After a ten-year run with the World Bank, he would find himself in Peru running for President — opposing the re-election of the Fujimori/Montesino criminal enterprise. Dr. Alejandro Toledo would win in 2001, making him the first Indigenous Native American in South America democratically elected to President in 500 years! In March 2002, President Toledo would persuade U.S. President George W. Bush to announce that the Peace Corps, after an absence of 27 years, would be returning to Peru, starting with 150 PCVs over the first 15 months.

Toledo's surprising success affirms the American belief that equal opportunity is a key condition for unleashing a society's human potential. Alejandro's rise to the Presidency is proof positive of the potency of the Peace Corps' grass-roots style of diplomacy. To embolden peasants to become Presidents, that is the work of the Peace Corps.

It is hard to believe an Andean shoeshine boy could rise to such academic heights. Alejandro, first of his family to attend a school, knew the importance of higher education. But he knew also that the opportunity he took advantage of would never have existed had not JFK started the Peace Corps, had not Mankiewicz sent PCVs into the barriadas to personally combat poverty, and had not PCVs from Nebraska and West Virginia reached out. Alejandro saw the creation of the Peace Corps as a brilliant stroke of statecraft:

> STATISTICALLY I didn't exist; I'm a statistical anomaly. If it had not been for JFK's Peace Corps and for America's higher education system, I would never have become President of Peru. JFK knew what he was doing. He planned to breakdown the walls that Fortress America had surrounded itself with in the 1950s by sending Peace Corps Volunteers abroad to engage in people-to-people interactions. No media, no govern-

ment, no cars, just diverse Americans reaching out to the world, showing America's humanity and demonstrating its spirit of generosity.

14

CAMPESINOS ALWAYS LOSE

1250–1533

Beginning in 1250 the Inca Empire ruled the Andean Mountain Range. Incas conquered and absorbed various cultures, like the Wari culture of the Mantaro Valley (500 CE–1000 CE) who were conquered and folded into the Inca Empire.

1533 — Spanish Colonization of the Inca Empire

It took less than 40 years for the Spanish, under the leadership of Captain Francisco Pizarro to take control of Peru.

It started with the execution of the last Incan emperor, Atahualpa, on 26th of July 1533, and ended on September 24, 1572 in Cusco's Plaza de Armas with the be-heading of Túpac Amaru (1545-1572) the last of the Incan monarchs. His execution was witnessed by 15,000 inhabitants.

Túpac Amaru, who was Sapa Inca (the only ruler of the Inca empire), had eluded capture in a jungle hideaway, and was finally captured, along with five of his generals, and taken to Cusco where the new Spanish Viceroy Don Francisco de Toledo ordered the generals hung. The Catholic clergy and inhabitants of Cusco wailed at Toledo's decree to behead Túpac Amaru.

Atahualpa, the last Inca Emperor — *Research Library, The Getty Research Institute*

Wealth for the colonizers

Spain's quest for riches in their newly created Virreinato del Peru (Viceroyalty of Peru) in 1542 was soon rewarded.

On April 1, 1545, a team of Spanish prospectors from Cusco, who were looking for minerals in the southern Andes (now part of Bolivia), discovered the 15,827-foot domed mountain of Potosí. Named Sumaq urqu (Beautiful Mountain), was where Huayna Capac (11th Inca) used small clay guayras (ovens) to extract silver from the mountain's rich iron-ore core, and there the prospectors stumbled on to Potosí's fabled Cerro Rico mine (rich mountain), the richest source of silver in human history.

Spain ramped up the extraction and drove the mine's development to unimagined heights. Initially, in the 16th-17th centuries, Cerro Rico produced over 60% of the world's silver. Mining Potosí's high-grade ore created fabulous wealth, attracting miners and entrepreneurs, artisans and food providers from around the world.

At the peak of the Colonial silver boom, Potosí was bursting with 200,000 inhabitants, and was the largest city in the Western Hemisphere. In a 1603 report, 58,000 Quechua-speaking Indigenous natives were working at Cerro Rico's legendary mine, which, over the centuries, exported more than 62,000 metric tons of silver.

Mining Potosí required massive numbers of miners. The Spaniards knew that the native workers resented dangerous mining practices and hence were not a reliable workforce. To get around that obstacle, the overlords enacted draconian forced-labor laws. Cynically, the Spanish used the exact same word the Incas used to build community — mit'a (donating work to a public works project or communal agriculture effort and sharing in its outcome), which in Spanish, translated as faena (minus the sharing part).

Diabolically, the Spaniards flipped the cooperative meaning of mit'a to one of forced manual labor. The Spanish mita system conscripted over 13,000 Quechua-speaking campesinos every year to work at the mine.

By the late 17th century, 50% of the adult population living between Cusco and La Paz had been decimated by the mining rigors of Potosí, where lethal mercury was then being used as its extraction agent.

Even African slaves from Brazil were sent to Argentina, transported across the Chaco Plains up to Bolivia and finally arriving at Cerro Rico de Potosí.

The deaths of miners, many scholars argue, may have numbered as many as eight million — including both Native American and African.

1780

Two hundred years later things became much worse for the Indigenous people of the altiplano.

In Tinta, oldest of all communities, there is an ancient wall that marks where the Inca Sun God Viracocha stopped on his journey from Lake Titicaca to Cusco.

On November 4, 1780, the highly respected Incan leader Condorcanqui made a request of El Corregidor Antonio de Arriaga, administrative leader of Tinta appointed by the Spanish king. He asked Arriaga, ". . . that alleviation of negative conditions be granted to the natives, the creoles, and mestizos."

Arriaga's arrogant answer provoked a rebellion, and on November 10, 1780, as he attempted to leave Tinta, he was pulled from his horse and murdered before a crowd of thousands.

Condorcanqui then took over the leadership of Tinta and assumed the name Túpac Amaru II. He was, as everyone knew, a legitimate Inca descendant — he was the great-grandson of Túpac Amaru, and had been educated in their ways by Jesuits.

Túpac Amaru II declared: "The end to the mita system and control of villages would be returned to Inca leaders, *caciques* (princes of the Inca Empire)."

Spain's military fought back, and called in reserves from as far away as Cartageña, Colombia, and in May of 1781 Túpac Amaru II and his wife, Michela Bastidas, his *mano derecha* (right arm) in battle, and one of their children, were captured. Tried in

Cusco's Plaza de Armas, he was sentenced to death by quartering, and his wife and child had their tongues cut out and then were beheaded. But on May 18th the extravaganza of quartering 43-year old Túpac Amaru II with four horses didn't work. Finally, the authorities just cut off his head, and that was the end of the 1780 Rebellion.

From that point on, the Viceroy forbade the speaking of the Quechua language and the wearing of Indigenous clothing; and the history of the Inca was to be forever obliterated, never again to be mentioned.

1826

Nevertheless, Túpac Amaru II's rebellion had precipitated the momentous Wars of Independence (1808–1826) that resulted in Spain being ejected from every one of their South America *Virreinatos* (Vice Royalties).

In 1826 Venezuelan liberator and military and political leader Simón Bolívar, in thanking those in Peru who made the struggle possible, singled out the importance of the female fighters of Túpac Amaru II's Rebellion of 1780 to 1782. (Centuries later Peruvian historians felt the Rebellion was so significant they celebrated its Bicentennial in 1980 with much hullabaloo.)

The End of Colonialism

In 1826 Spain had finally been ousted from its New World colony; and in flamboyant Potosí the hunt for silver was over. Its far less lucrative cousin of tin was now king.

In 1872 railroad tycoon Don Enrique Meiggs was contracted by the Peruvian caudillo government to build a rail line across the barren *altiplano* (plateau) from Cusco to Puno, a port on the northwest of Lake Titicaca. For Meiggs — "I lay track where llamas walk" — it was to be a straight-line 10-hour train trip, traveling between 11,200 feet and 12,648. He was also contracted to build a rail line south, from Juliaca, at 12,549 feet, a key crossroad of the Puno-Lake Titicaca region, down to Arequipa and across the desert plain to the port of Mollendo on the Pacific Ocean.

An early Peruvian locomotive

The Iron Horse, Meiggs promised, would jump-start Peru's export business, and the world would no longer have to wait for four-footed animals to deliver goods to the coast — the Iron Horse could deliver a thousand more ingots than any mule train.

The Ferrocarrill del Sur (Southern train line) from Cusco to Puno was 206 miles long, and except for the daily squeal of a passing train's iron wheels careening against the steel rails, the only sound on the altiplano was that of a soft wind. No birds chirping, no children laughing, no noise except at train stops where bedraggled children begged for coins as their mothers anxiously sold food to railroad passengers hanging out the windows.

The altiplano's silence continues to speak volumes about Peru's sordid past.

1960s
By the time the Peace Corps arrived in Peru in the early Sixties, Meiggs' train lines had been extended to mines in southwest-

ern Bolivia for transporting Potosí's silver booty to the outside world. But Potosí, the once vibrant, enormously wealthy, mining center, had become a two-bit tin mining community, and a severely polluted one. (UNESCO World Heritage Sites in Danger voted in 2015 to keep Potosí on its list of endangered sites due to its uncontrollable mining practices.)

Peru PCV Ron Arias (U. Washington, Nutrition 1963–1965) was among the first wave of Peace Corps Volunteers to arrive in country, and the nutrition program was a perfect way for the Peace Corps to begin working in poverty-stricken nations. Health and nutrition resources were non-existent for those living in the boonies of the Peruvian Andes.

Ron and his cohort nutritionist, PCV Mike Beede, were assigned to Sicuani, a train stop in the middle of the barren, brown Andean landscape, 99 miles south of Cusco, and 106 miles from Puno.

Ron, a community college transfer to UC Berkeley, in his first year had won a journalism scholarship to spend a year in Buenos Aires, Argentina, and having lived in Spain after WWII, he spoke excellent Spanish. In Buenos Aires, Ron had attended classes and submitted freelance articles to *AP* and the *Buenos Aires Herald*.

When his scholarship was completed he was not yet ready to return to academia.

PCV Ron Arias rides past the ruins of the Viracocha Walls.

Eager to see more of South America and having been inspired by JFK's call to help the poor, Arias volunteered for the Peace Corps.

Early in the morning of February 4, 1964, Ron and Mike left Sicuani to monitor the preparation for, and serving of, a new school lunch feeding program being started in the village of Cusipata that they were helping with.

They drove north toward Cusco in their small Food for Peace Jeep, following the bumpy pockmarked road that runs parallel to the rail line. As they approached the village of Tinta, they noticed hundreds of campesinos on the left side of the road who had just been evicted from their recently reclaimed farmlands.

On the right side of the road, they saw Guardia Civil officers and soldiers in green military uniforms setting up machine guns.

When the pop-pop-pop-pop sounds of gunfire registered on Ron, he hit the brakes and spun a half 'brodie' in the middle of the road and floor-boarded their pastel blue Jeep back toward Sicuani 17 kilometers away.

They stopped on the outskirts of their village at the hospital, and reported to the doctor on duty what they had just seen, and the doctor phoned the police.

The two PCVs then parked their little Jeep in the plaza to discuss the incident. They polished off some beers trying to understand what had just transpired.

A few hours later, surprised at how little public response there seemed to be to the massacre they had witnessed in Tinta, they returned to the hospital, which was right next to the train track.

There, parked on the hospital's rail spur, was a blood-soaked flatcar covered with dead bodies stacked like cordwood. Ron counted 17, including children.

The next day and the next day — and the next next day — no one seemed to have any memory of the massacre. Naturally, Ron, the budding journalist, couldn't believe the community-wide amnesia. "Don't know what you're talking about Sr. Arias."

In Lima the newspapers mainly missed the story.

Although international correspondent Norman Gall's "Letter from Peru" published in the June 1964 *Commentary Magazine* had the body count of a confrontation between Andean Native Americans and the police — the caudillo class — who took over the reins of government in 1826 from the disgraced Spanish. Gall wrote, "The Indians rioted."

Ron said, "They were protesting" eviction from their ancestral lands.

Whatever the reason, Indigenous people were killed and no one was held accountable.

Even after Ron had finished his term of service with the Peace Corps and returned to the U.S., he couldn't let go of the notion of no one caring. Eighteen months later, he published "Massacre in the Andes" in the September 25, 1965 issue of the *Christian Science Monitor*.

Ron was no cub reporter. He went on to report for *People Magazine* for two decades, often writing the popular "Up/Front" column, and since the 1964 Tinta Massacre, he's faced loaded guns numerous times in his career of covering international news breaking stories from Somalia to Sarajevo, from Kuwait to Haiti, from Nicaragua to Bosnia, one crisis after another — wars, earthquakes and famines.

The continuing struggle of the Campesinos

As we all know, the key to understanding the present resides in knowing the historical facts. Peace Corps training did not delve into the facts of Peru's awkward history of the Spanish conquest of the Inca Empire. It was too big a leap backwards to examine the long forgotten Inca culture. Like our Native Americans, all the Quechua-speaking people had to do was blend in — learn Spanish, cut their braids, and stop chewing wads of coca leaves.

The Indigenous people of Peru know their history, as do their more recent overlords, the caudillo military culture. What happened in Tinta was nothing new. The massacre echoed through history all the way back to the death of the last Inca, Sapa Inca (Only Inca).

The site of the Tinta massacre had been Hacienda Belenpampa, and its owners knew what was at stake. When confronted by hundreds of protesting campesinos, waving flags, and shouting slogans, they met the protesters with overwhelming force — government supplied machine-gun fire — killing and wounding dozens.

Given this grim history, commonly referred to in academia as "The Colonial Legacy," the February 4, 1964 Massacre at Tinta, ancient abode of Quechua-speaking Native Americans, was nothing new. It was another bloody chapter in the struggle of Inca Empire survivors to farm their ancestral lands, to live out their lives in peace.

PCV Mike Beede put the moment in perspective: "Stark eye-opening beginning in our effort to fathom Peru's deep divide between the powerful and the powerless. How would it be even possible for us to bridge those gaps?"

Ron wrote, "The falling women, wearing their colorful hand-woven skirts, looked like parachutes being blown across the windswept grasses of the altiplano."

They were gone, but their struggle for survival was not forgotten. It was all part of the daily battle to exist that Inca descendants have faced for centuries.

15

BROWN POWER

Living in such a remote location in Peru, Ron was grateful that out of the more than 400 Peace Corps Volunteers and staff members in-country, "the only other Mexican American I ever met or knew about was Ralph Guzmán." And Ron was glad he knew him.

When Guzmán's service on Peace Corps/Peru staff ended in the Fall of 1965, he returned to his doctoral studies at UCLA, and became the only Spanish-surnamed researcher (out of 3) of a gargantuan $647,999, multi-year (1964–71) Mexican American Study Project (MASP) funded by the Ford Foundation. It was a movement defining effort.

After completing his volunteer service, Ron was determined to earn his B.A., and he re-connected with Guzmán at UCLA. They reminisced about their extensive travels throughout South America, lapping up Latino culture. Both men admitted to one another how the Peace Corps had opened them up to the wonders and the wilds of that continent, and how the experience had instilled a pride within them that they had never felt before.

Ralph put Ron to work on the MASP, coding interview data on IBM punch cards for data processing. "Later, Ralph let me conduct interviews in East L.A. The experience completely transformed me." (It would later inspire his 1973 satirical play, "The Interview." In 1975 he published *The Road to Tamazunchale*, which was based on his experience as a PCV. It was a well-received novel — nominated for a National Book Award — infused with "magical realism," and set in L.A. and Peru.)

Ron saw Ralph as having "one foot in with the elites and one foot in the streets, comfortable in both." He felt Ralph had a comprehensive plan for righting wrongs, for battling poverty and income inequality, all the while raising cultural awareness. "He'd ask me, 'Are you Mexican American, or are you something else, something new, like a Chicano?'" Guzmán was an alchemist transforming the volatile tensions of the community into something new and positive.

Even before the MASP was completed, the Chicano Movement had become an equal partner of the diverse world of Mexican Americans, Hispanics, and Latinos, not to mention red, white and blue patriots and the down and out oppressed migratory workers. Each group had its fierce supporters, revealing sharp conflicts and the dire need for unity, and the one man who helped bring them all together, maybe not in name but definitely in spirit, was Ralph C. Guzmán, WWII combat vet, savvy community organizer, newsman, and skilled UCLA researcher.

Ralph Guzmán
UCSC
Special Collections

In the mid '60s he began to examine the Vietnam death records of Spanish-surnamed fatalities from five Southwestern states. He soon discovered that Mexican Americans constituted 19.2% of the war's fatalities yet they only comprised 11.9% of the total population, meaning they were dying at a rate 60% greater than what they represent in the population.

Before his study on fatalities was even published, Guzmán and his CSO ally, Congressman Edward Roybal, both WWII vets, and related by Ralph having married Roybal's niece, had already raised peoples' consciousness to the degree that the pride of dying in Vietnam suddenly was a symbol of victimization. A defining characteristic of Mexican American culture, the brave warrior, virtually changed overnight. They went from being America's loyal soldier to an exploited minority. It was a staggering intellectual accomplishment. It was also like lighting a fuse on a highly charged, highly combustible community aching for equality.

Prior to Ralph's monumental research on Mexican American society being published, the message was out. Guzmán, as a co-principal investigator of what in 1971 would be called "The Mexican American People: America's Second Largest Minority," had become an intellectual leader of the Chicano Movement. He even directed his inquiry toward Anglos, publishing think pieces about "Brown Power."

On at least one trip to D.C. in 1967 to reconnoiter with Mankiewicz, Guzmán met with Senator Kennedy in his office. He spoke to Kennedy of the growing influence of Mexican American college student leadership, pointing to how many of them had recently been elected Student Body Presidents at L.A. colleges, long the domain of privileged Anglos. And they only account for 4% of the student population, Guzmán no doubt argued. He sensed a rising awareness amongst the youth, and urged the Senator to meet with United Mexican American Students (UMAS) the next time he was in L.A.

The second week in November, Mankiewicz called Guzmán to say the Senator would meet with his UMAS campus leaders for breakfast in two days . . . Veteran's Day.

For the meeting, Guzmán chose Lucy's El Adobe Restaurant on 5536 Melrose Avenue — the owners, Frank & Lucy Casado, were longtime supporters of MAPA (Mexican American Political Association). Now a political science professor at Cal State L.A., Professor Guzmán spread the word to a dozen UMAS leaders: "RFK was coming to meet and to talk strategy."

RFK was coming indeed, but he was majorly grumpy. In fact, he had fallen off the public radar following the soul-searching week of November 1–7 discussing with his family and friends about whether he should run for the Presidency in '68. They met in Manhattan, they met in D.C., and they met in Hickory Hill. Almost everyone was against the idea and felt '72 was safer, although the Senator and his aides anxiously wondered if the Nation could last that long.

Alberto Juárez, the titular "chair" of UMAS chapters, remembered watching RFK walking with Guzmán toward Lucy's, "He had a swagger. He looked like he had been up all night and had just flown into town."

Alberto, a recent Navy vet, wasn't the only ex-military man sitting around the breakfast table at Lucy's, four of the twelve were. During the breakfast, he remembered how somber and business-like RFK was.

The Chicano community newspaper *La Raza* reported in the 11/15/67 edition that Kennedy listened carefully as the student leaders expressed their complaints, "The top two being police brutality and the failure of education. The new sense of identity as 'Chicanos' dominated the conversation." Kennedy hardly spoke. In the end, RFK told them, "Real change won't come from Washington. That you will have to do yourselves."

Alberto recalled, "He told us we would have to make the changes that we wanted to see through organizing, by raising issues. RFK had a steely look. You could tell he was a seasoned organizer. To run his brother's campaign for the Senate and for the Presidency you would have to know a lot about communities and about developing them into taking collective action."

The only rule for the meeting had been "No Media," but somehow it was broken. *La Raza* reported that a KHJ-TV reporter suddenly showed up for an impromptu interview. Alberto could not believe how fast RFK transformed himself from a somber, street-savvy tough into a smiling media-friendly politician, "Night-to-Day in a flash."

The newscaster asked RFK if he was planning on meeting the President, who was arriving at El Toro Marine Base in the afternoon. "No," RFK answered curtly, dismissively ending the unscheduled Interview.

Ever since LBJ's Century City fundraising debacle in June, the President had been unable to appear in public for fear of hearing the chant, "Hey, Hey, LBJ, how many kids . . . ?" The TV reporter reminded the television audience, "Today the President is visiting three military bases as he flies across country."

The bottom-line of Kennedy's 11/11/67 Veteran's Day meeting: UMAS decided not to get involved in any Anglo campaigns. They felt, though, that their meeting with a national leader like Kennedy acknowledged the growing power they had. How to use that power was the issue.

Guzmán, the veteran activist, was working many channels. He had to be pleased, though. *La Raza* contained a display ad celebrating: "Twenty Years of CSO Support of the Community." Twenty years before, back in 1947 as a 22-year-old WWII vet, Guzmán helped to form CSO as East L.A.'s home base "for mutual aid, community services, and civic action." Twenty years later, CSO was still on the point of the spear. There were now 34 chapters.

At Cal State L.A.'s 50th Anniversary celebration of its Department of Chicano Studies (9/6/2010), UFW co-founder Dolores Huerta in her Inaugural Lecture gave CSO all the credit for the Chicano Movement's success; she also named the City of Los Angeles as the birthplace of the Chicano Movement.

After a 90-minute breakfast, Kennedy left for a "Palm Springs vacation."

The last half of November was jammed: the 17th — Kennedy Family's donation to the Smithsonian Institution of "Caroline," the family airplane; the 26th — publication of his book, *To Seek A Newer World*, based in part on his November 1965 Trip to South America; the 27th — *Face The Nation* TV interview; and, at the end of the month, a meeting at the capitol with U.S. Senator Eugene McCarthy of Minnesota.

16

NOT A ONE-ISSUE CANDIDATE

As an honorably discharged veteran, having completed my 8-year obligation (1957–1965), I was under no threat of having to serve in Vietnam. Select Service had re-classified me as 4A, meaning I would only be drafted after all the women and children had been called up.

But as a recent veteran of the June 23rd Century City Anti-Vietnam War march and resulting police riot, I realized I had to become more involved in ending the Vietnam War. It was destroying America, which, according to Thomas Jefferson, was the world's last best chance for creating a place on Earth safe for everyone.

Through one of my KELP drinking buddies, now a young lawyer at the high-powered O'Melveny & Myers law firm, I wrangled an invitation to a conference of California Democratic Party activists led by Warren Christopher (Secretary of State under Bill Clinton), Richard Sherwood (LACMA trustee), and Victor Palmieri (Deputy Director, Kerner Commission Report on U.S. urban rioting of 1967).

Dismayed by actor Ronald Reagan's November 1966 victory over their ally, Governor Edmund "Pat" Brown, these heavyweight activists planned to re-group and to inject some young blood into their experienced cadre. They called themselves the Committee for California.

Their "Let Us Begin Anew" conference, so named by Sherwood, was held in mid-November in downtown Los Angeles to unite party activists, but blew-up over the war. Attendees were divided between stopping the war and supporting the President. Before leaving, I gave one of the anti-Vietnam War activists my UCLA business card and told him to call me if Senator Kennedy enters the race.

By the end of 1967, U.S. troop strength had reached almost 500,000! Anti-war marches had become larger than what the police could control. The March on the Pentagon on the 21st of October drew over 100,000 protesters — the largest anti-war demonstration in American history.

The insanity of the Vietnam War had to be stopped. Leaders had their heads in the sand. LBJ's Great Society was in the toilet. People were rioting in the streets, burning down local businesses. We were at war with ourselves.

I had been raised since birth to be an American warrior. As a youngster I awoke every morning to the sounds of World War II troops marching through the streets of Camp Miami Beach, counting out their manly cadences before the sun had even risen. I saw planes crash, ships burn — all from the palm tree-lined shores of Collins Avenue.

All through the late 1940s we youngsters in Berdoo re-lived WWII hand-to-hand combat battles with the enemy. We fought in heavily pockmarked terrain where serene orange groves were being radically transformed into housing tracts for California's new arrivals. We even devised tortures for captured enemy soldiers.

As soon as I graduated from high school I signed up for active-duty military service. My college book collection on "War" won 4th prize in the Campbell Book Store's annual UCLA Student Book Collection competition. My favorite tome was the U.S. Army's large-format, softcover 1961 *Green Beret/Special Forces Manual for Fighting Wars of National Liberation.*

My minor, as a political science major, was nuclear defense; and my nuclear war mentor, Dr. Bernard Brodie, cautioned, "You never want to fight a land war 10,000 miles away when all the enemy has to do is to walk across the road."

The 1962 Cuban Missile Crisis never worried Dr. Brodie, who was also on the staff of The RAND Corporation, a U.S. government-financed "think tank" in neighboring Santa Monica. He was long considered the "Father of Nuclear Détente" for his seminal 1959 treatise "Strategy in the Missile Age," and believed the Soviet Union would never go to war over Cuba. "Cuba is too close to the U.S.; despite intercontinental ballistics," Dr. Brodie explained in October of 1962 to our political science seminar, "Nuclear Defense Strategies"... "geographic proximity is one of the immutable rules that govern international relations."

Dr. Brodie, considered by many theorists as the "American Clauswitz of the Atomic Age," added the intellectual element to my warrior portfolio. He had our seminar of a dozen-plus Bruins read what all the RAND theorists were proposing: Hermann Kahn's two books, *On Thermonuclear War* and *Thinking About the Unthinkable*, Albert Wohlstetter's *Delicate Balance of Terror*, Thomas Schelling's *The Strategy of Conflict*, and Henry Kissinger's *Necessity of Choice*. It was in this manner that we learned about "deterrence," "proliferation," "mutually assured destruction" (MAD), and the prospects of a nuclear winter.

The Kennedy Brothers had learned many lessons about war and warriors from the Cuban Missile Crisis of 1962 that had triggered a 13-day nuclear war standoff with the Soviet Union. At the core was the realization that war was not an extension of politics; war was the end of politics. Hence, their push in the summer of 1963 for "a strategy of peace."

Amidst the Thanksgiving weekend distractions of 1967, President Johnson quietly replaced his Secretary of Defense Robert McNamara with Clark Clifford, a Washington insider of a more hawkish disposition. LBJ sent McNamara, architect of the Vietnam War who was starting to doubt the War's spiraling trajectory, off to Europe to head the World Bank.

Translation: McNamara was fired; he was now out of sight, out of mind. As a consequence, the decision-making apparatus for the entire Vietnam War shrunk to a troika — LBJ, Secretary of State Dean Rusk, and the military's Chairman of the Joint Chiefs of Staff General Earle Wheeler . . . not the U.S. Congress.

The Senate's Special Sub-Committee on Indian Education met January 4th 1968 at San Francisco's American Indian House to hear California Indian leaders' input on improving the deplorable education they had been receiving from the state of California. Senator Robert Kennedy, Chairman of the Sub-Committee, asked Native American leadership for the facts; and the stories of institutional failures followed, as well as their proposed solutions.

Recoiling from the gravitas of the defeated Native Americans still struggling to exist under United States rule, Robert Kennedy, at the end of the day, when speaking at The Commonwealth Club, shifted gears. Leaving behind the mundane task of educating the vanquished, he explored the more soul-searching question of: What do we, the victors, stand for?

Typically, Kennedy began lightheartedly:

> I'M PLEASED to be here. I'm out here to hold some hearings on Indian affairs; and to ensure that there is no effort to and no success in the "Draft Kennedy" movement taking place here in the state of California. I think my brother Teddy is much too young to run for president of the United States.

As a political animal, Kennedy couched his "what do we stand for" argument in terms of the upcoming presidential election:

> We must look not only to immediate crises but also to the nature and the direction of the civilization that we wish to build, that we wish to take part in . . .. The mastery of transient events, our accomplishments, our victories will matter far less than what we contribute — all of us in this country — to the liberation of the human spirit. It will depend on whether we act . . ..

And RFK then listed one ethical issue after another — money, fairness, power; then concluded with:

To MEET and master these challenges will take great
vision and take great persistence . . . but the larger question of whether we have advanced our civilization and
the cause of freedom will depend on our own morality,
on our philosophy, on our commitment to our ideals
and to us.

As if in response to these ethical challenges, 1968 violently exploded, producing a torrent of uncontrollable forces that
changed U.S. policy both at home and abroad.

At home, U.S. Senator Eugene McCarthy of Minnesota was
challenging President Johnson in the New Hampshire Democratic Party's March 12th Presidential Primary.

From afar, the Viet Cong's surprise Tet Offensive in late January hugely discredited LBJ's rosy version of, "Vietnam carrying
its weight."

On the 31st of January, 245 American soldiers were killed,
the largest daily loss of life during the entire war!

Viet Cong successes in Hue, the district capitol, and the
grinding jungle battle for neighboring villages lasted throughout the month of February with huge human losses suffered by
all sides — Vietnamese villagers, South Vietnam soldiers, Viet
Cong, and the American invaders.

The televised account of this mayhem was ugly, dishearten-
ing, and shameful. *LIFE Magazine* always had the most soulful
color photos of American soldiers dying. The photos made you
weep.

The repugnant war kept going on. All of this killing and destruction was to become the new norm. More families would
suffer. Internally, our nation was bleeding to death.

The Tet Offensive that began on January 31, 1968 revealed
that at the heart of America's military failures resided a repugnant ally. On February 1st an Associated Press photographer
captured in one image how the Vietnam conflict had devolved
into a barbaric war; on February 2nd that grotesque photo ran
on the front page of every newspaper in the world! The chief of

South Vietnam's national police boldly executed a "guerrilla" in the streets of Saigon with a pistol shot to the head of a civilian wearing a plaid short-sleeved sport shirt, his hands cuffed behind him. The AP wire-photo caption enhanced the horror of the image, "The guerrilla grimaces at the impact of the bullet in this picture . . .."

The chief explained, "The Viet Cong killed many Americans and many of my people." This audacious street murder of a prisoner, hands cuffed behind his back, pushed many law-abiding Americans to oppose this Wild West war in Asia that was being waged in their name.

The February 29th publication of the much anticipated Kerner Commission's Report on the urban violence that ravaged America in 1967: Its studied exploration into the causes of over 75 urban riots (racism and an unfair distribution of governmental resources), and their thoughtful recommendations for the future (hire more Negroes, community policing, involve universities) were summarily ignored by LBJ.

His denial further polarized voters, and boosted McCarthy's prospects in New Hampshire where, on March 12, 1968, McCarthy lost to the President 42% (23,263) to LBJ's 49% (27,520) by 4,257. This did not include 2,000 write-in votes, of which Senator Robert Kennedy received the most (606).

Now that RFK wouldn't be blamed for the split in the Democratic Party, he jumped into the race feet first. His entry triggered a political earthquake that rocked the establishment from coast to coast. A tsunami of public interest in his candidacy shot across the landscape in lightning speed, daily gaining momentum.

Mankiewicz joked to RFK that they were finally, "Free at last."

Even so, JFK Library Archives: Oral History (OH) records show that on March 8th key Kennedy Senatorial aide John Nolan, a Marine veteran and D.C. activist-lawyer who worked for both JFK and RFK during the Kennedy Administration, selected Bill Norris to be Senator Kennedy's California campaign manager. He was the activist-attorney I had spoken with at the "Let Us Begin Anew" conference the previous November. Nolan and Norris had met in D.C. in the 1950s when they were law clerks to U.S. Supreme Court Justices Tom Clark and William Douglas respectively. Norris was a player in Democratic Party state politics, a Princeton grad, Stanford Law Review. He, too, was the son of a coal miner.

On March 10th, Senator Kennedy flew to Delano, heart of the mammoth San Joaquin Valley cornucopia, to join farmworker-activist César Chávez, co-founder of NFW, in breaking his 25-day water-only fast to dramatize migrant farmworkers' rights to organize.

Andy Imutan, co-founder, Agricultural Workers Organizing Committee (AWOC), Dolores Huerta, co-founder, National Farm Workers Organizing Committee (NFWOC), Larry Itliong, co-founder, Agricultural Workers Organizing Committee (AWOC) and RFK at a rally in Delano, California before the breaking of Cesar Chavez's 25 day fast, also co-founder, National Farm Worker Organizing Committee (NFWOC). March 10, 1968 (#319) *Walter P. Reuther Library, Archives of Labor and Urban Affairs, Wayne State University.*

Originally trained in Saul Alinsky's style of confrontational community organizing, Chávez had by now developed a Gandhi-infused belief in non-violent social protest. Weakened by his loss of 35 lbs., César had called for the end to his fast in support of non-violent protest on Sunday. A crowd of 8,000 had gathered to greet Senator Robert Kennedy. Some in the crowd yelled, "Run Robert Run." He and César went to Mass and took Communion together. They were the same height, the same tenacious breed. RFK admitted he liked César, and the farmworkers never stopped loving him.

After Mass, Kennedy praised Chávez for his compassion and his courage in publicly extolling his belief in non-violent protest, "Let me say that violence is no answer . . . where there is violence our nation loses. Violence destroys far more than it can ever create."

NFW co-founder Dolores Huerta shared the stage with RFK that day. She saw the far-reaching impact RFK's visit had on the boycott, "He put our effort on the front page of the national news, that the Senator from New York came all the way to Delano, California to be there with César."

As fast as he had arrived, Robert Kennedy flew back east for a series of meetings at his home in McLean, Virginia.

The deep rumblings of discontent that Professor Guzmán had sensed amongst the youth of Southern California exploded at the exact same time RFK and César were breaking his fast.

But the explosion was not amongst the college students. Rather, the out-in-the-street rebellion came from East L.A.'s high school youth — led by Lincoln High School teacher Sal Castro, an early Chicano Movement organizer. The well-organized BlowOuts at a half dozen L.A. high schools over inferior education blew hard for the month of March, resulting in massive confrontations with the L.A. County Sheriffs, LAPD arrests, media madness, meetings with the LA Unified School District board, and, eventually, changes . . . small ones.

These two disparate elements — NFW support of impoverished migratory farm workers in the San Joaquin Valley, and the East L.A. high school BlowOuts decrying astonishingly high dropout rates of high school students — were simultaneous expressions of Mexican American fury at a society that treated them as second class citizens.

In this caldron of social protest, the Chicano Movement became the face of their broad-based resentment. *Los Angeles Times* [3/17/68] headlines screamed "Brown Power," and reported that UCLA Professor Ralph Guzmán said the Blow-Outs reminded him of the Indian riots in Cusco in 1963 when he was serving with the Peace Corps in Peru. The Spanish-surnamed world of California had spontaneously joined in full protest against their Anglo overlords.

Behind the scenes, Dolores and César unleashed their farmworker troops. The strike was temporarily put on hold and hundreds of farmworker pickets were sent into Latino neighborhoods around the state to campaign for Robert Kennedy. Here was their chance to exercise the organizing clout they had developed over the past three years promoting a national boycott. Their mission was to register people to vote and to convince them to vote for Robert Kennedy. They slept in churches, barns, stables, and on the living room floors of compatriots. They all had heard Robert Kennedy in Delano, reminding them, "that when you're old and bent from many years of labor, no man will stand taller than you when you say, 'I marched with César'."

Dolores, long an advocate of Fred Ross's style of home-based organizing, spelled out their battle plan: "Our strategy was to go door-to-door to find people who would be precinct captains. We'd leave them with a list of registered voters and ask them to convince their neighbors to vote for Kennedy. We'd wait a couple of days and come back to make sure they were really doing it. And if not, then we would take the list and go to another house."

On March 15th, Norris called to tell me that he and Nolan were at the International Hotel next door to LAX.

I knew exactly where they were. On June 13, 1964 Marie and I spent our wedding night in the Bridal Suite and opened all of our wedding gifts before flying off the next morning to New York, and Peace Corps Training at Cornell University.

Inside the suite of hotel rooms, I discovered California power brokers battling over the leadership of the Democratic Party delegation pledged to Kennedy. Mervyn Dymally, Trinidadian-born State Senator, was bitter in losing to Carmen Warschaw, Jesse Unruh's wealthy conservative ally. Dymally had been a coordinator for JFK's 1960 Presidential campaign in California; and in 1966 he was the 1st African American ever elected to the California State Senate. Warschaw, often referred to as "The Dragon Lady," was allied with "Big Daddy" Unruh, the rotund Speaker of California's State Assembly, who had a statewide presence intimated by his California-sized belly. Senator Dymally's influence was primarily in South Central.

Soon afterwards, Kennedy for President Campaign headquarters opened up in the Miracle Mile section of Los Angeles at the northeast corner of Hauser and Wilshire Boulevards.

The Kennedy Campaign had now materialized. I was stoked about the prospects for peace. I had misgivings, though, regarding the courage of my fellow UCLA graduates and how committed they might be to stopping the Vietnam War.

Two days before the June 23rd Century City protest, Marie and I had called 20 former UCLA classmates who we hadn't seen since our June 1964 marriage in the Pacific Palisades and immediate departure into the Peace Corps. We invited them to an Anti-Vietnam War poster-making party at our Westwood duplex and then to join us the following day in the one-mile march from Rancho Park to Century City.

Only two of our UCLA friends accepted our protest poster-making party invite, plus D.J. Boyd, a PCV we met in Peru who was now a UCLA graduate student of anthropology. The other eighteen Bruins had excuses, most too lame to repeat. Young lawyers fresh out of law school, who were now assistant district attorneys and assistant federal prosecutors apologized that they could not join in. As one young UCLA Law School graduate explained: "Participating in the protest march would mean taking a chance on getting a ding on my record and prevent me someday from becoming a judge, when I'd really be able to protect the citizenry."

Already sounding like a veteran lawyer he summed up his inability to attend: "In the broad scheme of things my singular participation in the protest isn't worth the potential damage that could be done to my life-long career. *Capiche?*"

The protest march having been shut down by an "LAPD Riot" was, on a certain level, to be expected. Southern California was a White, Anglo-Saxon, Protestant refuge with Deep South roots that spawned conservative Los Angeles, including Mayor Sam Yorty, head-bashing LAPD, Red-baiting U.S. Congressman Richard Nixon, and the reactionary John Birch Society of Pasadena that believed "Supreme Court Chief Justice Earl Warren (from Northern California) is a Communist." Add to that, the gross scene of publicly financed bureaucrats (policemen) illegally beating peaceful unarmed citizens with Billy clubs was disgraceful, cowardly, and un-American. That whole ugly scene, however, revealed a source of cowardice I had not imagined.

The lack of courage exhibited by these newly-minted college graduates, from one of America's elite public universities, made Robert Kennedy's entrance into the Vietnam War dispute all the more significant.

Kennedy was not a one-issue candidate like McCarthy. He had a fully developed agenda of issues, programs, and policies that he stood for. He could engage the whole nation — urban and rural. The challenge Kennedy faced was to break through the lies and denials of the Johnson Administration; and he did this by demanding from himself a level of honesty that transcended politics as we all knew it.

"It is quite unusual to have a second chance to materialize your desire," the sage Buson noted. Indeed, when a man's dreams have been dashed and he's suddenly given a second chance to realize them, he'll dig deep into his core to make sure that he stands for the truth — a truth that makes sense to all.

On March 16th Senator Robert Kennedy announced his candidacy for the Presidency in the same Senate caucus room his older brother Jack had used on January 2nd 1960 to announce his Presidential ambitions:

> I RUN BECAUSE I am convinced that this country is on a perilous course and I have such strong feelings about what must be done that I am obliged to do all I can. I run to seek new policies — policies to close the gaps between black and white, rich and poor, young and old, in this country and around the world.

RFK concluded:

> I do not lightly dismiss the dangers and difficulties of challenging an incumbent President; but these are not ordinary times and this is not an ordinary election. At stake is not simply the leadership of our party or even our country — it is our right to moral leadership on this planet.

RFK celebrated St. Patrick's Day politicking through the state of New York from Albany to Brooklyn, where he boarded a commercial flight and began his first cross-country trip in pursuit of the Presidency. Instead of starting off in a Democratic stronghold like Boston or Chicago, Kennedy headed straight into Middle America and the Deep South: two university stops in Kansas, Vanderbilt University in Nashville, and University of Alabama in Tuscaloosa.

He would be returning to Alabama almost five years to the day in 1963, when as Attorney General, he had battled Governor George Wallace over the "right of Negro students to attend University of Alabama." Wallace was a formidable politician who loomed large over the entire political landscape. He had been elected governor in January of 1963 running on the racist platform: "Segregation Now, Segregation Today, and Segregation Ta'marrah."

The private 82-minute conversation between RFK and Wallace on April 25, 1963 ended in a stalemate, and did not deter Wallace seven weeks later from initially blocking the Foster Auditorium doorway to integration at the University of Alabama. Later in the day, faced with a subpoena and no TV cameras present, Wallace caved to U.S. Deputy Attorney General Nicholas Katzenbach.

17

JFK ON CIVIL RIGHTS

Govenor Wallace's infamous stand for segregation was made on June 11, 1963, the day of my graduation from UCLA, and the day after JFK proposed his heroic strategy for world peace to the graduates of American University. Infuriated by Wallace's actions, President Kennedy angrily responded by declaring desegregation was a legal matter as well as a "moral issue." Immediately he scheduled a televised address from the Oval Office, "regarding Alabama and Negro civil rights."

Time was short. There was only one draft of his speech and only two saw it: Ted Sorenson, Special Counsel and chief speechwriter, and his brother Attorney General Robert Kennedy. Civil rights had been ruminating inside the President. The time had come; with or without a finished typed speech, he knew what he wanted to say.

That evening President John Kennedy in addressing the nation argued that Negroes needed their civil rights to be equal to everyone else's and that the Nation needed to correct the civil wrongs done to them.

THIS AFTERNOON, following a series of threats and defiant statements, the presence of Alabama National Guardsmen was required on the University of Alabama to carry out the final and unequivocal order of the United States District Court of the Northern District of Alabama. That order called for the admission of two clearly qualified young Alabama residents who happened to have been born Negro.

That they were admitted peacefully on the campus is due in good measure to the conduct of the students of the University of Alabama, who met their responsibilities in a constructive way.

157

. . .

This Nation was founded by men of many nations
and backgrounds. It was founded on the principle that
all men are created equal, and that the rights of every
man are diminished when the rights of one man are
threatened.

. . .

This is not a sectional issue. Difficulties over segregation and discrimination exist in every city, in every State
of the Union, producing in many cities a rising tide of
discontent that threatens the public safety. Nor is this a
partisan issue. In a time of domestic crisis men of good
will and generosity should be able to unite regardless of
party or politics. This is not even a legal or legislative issue alone. It is better to settle these matters in the courts
than on the streets, and new laws are needed at every
level, but law alone cannot make men see right.

We are confronted primarily with a moral issue. It is
as old as the scriptures and is as clear as the American
Constitution.

The heart of the question is whether all Americans
are to be afforded equal rights and equal opportunities,
whether we are going to treat our fellow Americans as
we want to be treated.

. . .

Now the time has come for this Nation to fulfill its
promise. The events in Birmingham and elsewhere have
so increased the cries for equality that no city or State
or legislative body can prudently choose to ignore them.

The fires of frustration and discord are burning in every city, North and South, where legal remedies are not
at hand. Redress is sought in the streets, in demonstrations, parades, and protests, which create tensions and
threaten violence and threaten lives.

We face, therefore, a moral crisis as a country and as
a people. It cannot be met by repressive police action. It

cannot be left to increased demonstrations in the streets. It cannot be quieted by token moves or talk. It is time to act in the Congress, in your State and local legislative body and, above all, in all of our daily lives.

. . .

A great change is at hand, and our task, our obligation, is to make that revolution, that change, peaceful and constructive for all.

Those who do nothing are inviting shame as well as violence. Those who act boldly are recognizing right as well as reality.

. . .

I am, therefore, asking the Congress to enact legislation giving all Americans the right to be served in facilities, which are open to the public — hotels, restaurants, theaters, retail stores, and similar establishments.

This seems to me to be an elementary right. Its denial is an arbitrary indignity that no American in 1963 should have to endure, but many do.

. . .

But legislation, I repeat, cannot solve this problem alone. It must be solved in the homes of every American in every community across our country.

In this respect I want to pay tribute to those citizens North and South who have been working in their communities to make life better for all. They are acting not out of a sense of legal duty but out of a sense of human decency.

After describing the disproportionate allocation of public resources that left Negro schools and communities at a huge disadvantage, President Kennedy asked, how could we be the champions of freedom and refuse to give all of our citizens equal rights and opportunities? One cannot legislate human decency, the President acknowledged. But that was at the core of the

problem, an absence of respect, of fairness, of human kindness.
Decency seemed to be beyond the grasp of some people, as if
they couldn't empathize. Was it perhaps a genetic deficiency?
Or was making money really the core of their anti-equality argument?

The President concluded:

> W E HAVE A RIGHT to expect that the Negro commu-
> nity will be responsible, will uphold the law, but they
> have a right to expect that the law will be fair, that the
> Constitution will be color blind . . .. This is what we are
> talking about and this is a matter which concerns this
> country and what it stands for; and in meeting that task I
> ask the support of all our citizens.

In two consecutive days, President Kennedy had fleshed out two
key elements of his New Frontier agenda: a worldwide strategy
for peace coupled to a domestic plan for ensuring and protecting
the civil rights of all citizens — peace and freedom.

The entire episode, from Alabama to the White House, was
filmed by Robert Drew as a documentary, *Crisis: Behind A
Presidential Commitment*, and was the first filmed scenes of a
U.S. President in action.

Just after midnight, on June 12th, and before anyone could ap-
plaud JFK's dramatic civil rights address, NAACP's Mississippi
field secretary Medgar Evers was ambushed in front of his home
in Jackson — shot in the heart from behind.

When the summer of 1963 began, two diametrically opposed
forces were locked in a deadly battle for America's body and soul.

By the end of the year, LBJ had transformed JFK's strategy
of peace into a land war in Southeast Asia; despite the legal
eradication of segregation in America racism continued unapol-
ogetically.

18

A FORCE ON THE STUMP

Five years later, as RFK embarked on his 1968 Campaign for the Presidency, he wanted to know the depth of his support in the Heartland.

Adam Walinsky, his speechwriter and Senate aide, claimed to reporters the campaign hit the ground running.

As a U.S. Senator RFK had worked on all the key issues: employment, poverty, gun control, nuclear arms reduction, malnutrition, juvenile delinquency, criminal justice, and urban sprawl, and he had developed programmatic responses that he tested and re-tested with numerous experts. He had all that information inside him; he was raring to go, and up to the task.

He did not cajole audiences; he challenged them.

The wild scene at Kansas State University's arena in Manhattan KS took the Kennedy team by surprise. The building was jammed to its metal rafters with over 14,000 students. Everyone clapping hands in unison gave the place the feel of an old-fashioned revival meeting. It was the largest crowd in campus history.

There had been inklings the night before when their plane stopped in Kansas City that a positive reception was brewing. Later in the night, in Topeka, they were met by welcoming crowds hoisting handmade signs ordering him to, "Sock it to 'em, Bobby," as the popular TV show *Rowan & Martin's Laugh-In* weekly urged an angry nation.

The invitation to speak at KSU had been made months before and was to focus on poverty and income inequality.

He was to give the Landon Lecture named in honor of Alf Landon, former Kansas GOP Governor and Presidential candidate.

Senator Robert Kennedy opened his Presidential Campaign fearlessly broaching the elephant in the room with his speech, "Ending the Vietnam War:"

. . .

I AM WILLING TO BEAR my share of the responsibility, before history and before my fellow citizens. But past error is no excuse for its perpetuation. Tragedy is a tool for the living to gain wisdom, not a guide by which to live by. Now as ever, we do ourselves best justice when we measure ourselves against ancient tests, and a good man yields when he knows his course is wrong, and re-pairs the evils. The only sin is pride.

. . .

If it becomes necessary to destroy all of South Vietnam in order to save it, will we do that too, and if we care so little about South Vietnam that we are willing to see the land destroyed and its people dead, then why are we there in the first place?"

The building exploded in applause.

All wars take their toll, but the costs of the war's present course far outweigh anything we can reasonably hope to gain by it, for ourselves or for the people of Vietnam. It must be ended, and in my judgment, it can be ended.

. . .

I come here today, to this great university, to ask your help; not for me, but for your country and for the peo-ple of Vietnam.

Thunderous applause electrified the arena!
You are the people, as President Kennedy said, who have "the least ties to the present and the greatest stake in the future."

...

Our country is in danger: not just from foreign enemies; but above all, from our own misguided policies – and what they can do to the Nation that Thomas Jefferson once said was the last, best hope of man. There is a contest on, not for the rule of America, but for the heart of America. In these next eight months, we are going to decide what this country will stand for – and what kind of men we are.

...

I ask you, as tens of thousands of young men and women are doing all over this land, to organize yourselves and then to go forth and work for new policies not just in Southeast Asia, but here at home as well, so that we have a new birth for this country, a new light to guide us. And I pledge to you, if you will give me your help, if you will give me your hand, I will work for you and we will have a New America!

Again the crowd erupted into wild cheering and thundering applause.

During the question-and-answer period, Kennedy's wit sparkled. An apologetic voice asked, "Put yourself in President Johnson's position . . . .."

To wit RFK interjected, in his signature Bostonian accent, "That's what I'm trying to do."

Stamping and screaming, the audience roared back its approval.

Veteran *LOOK Magazine* photographer Stanley Tetrick screamed over the din to Kennedy staffers, "This is Kansas. Fucking Kansas! RFK is going all the fucking way!"

Four hours down the road at Kansas University in Lawrence, there was an even larger crowd — 20,000 foot-stomping students, faculty and others — met the candidate and his entourage.

Not a bad turnout considering KU student registration was only 16,000.

By the time the candidate entered the overflowing Phineas Allen Fieldhouse the crowd was chanting and clapping in rhythm. It was the largest audience in campus history and that includes KU's NCAA Basketball Championship led by Wilt Chamberlain.

RFK's speech, "Recapturing America's Moral Vision," quickly included elements of his Vietnam War speech because the KSU audience had responded so enthusiastically to its End the War message. His focus, though, was on materialism and he utilized the economic measurement of Gross National Product (GNP) to expose the hollowness of defining national progress through the accumulation of material goods:

I RUN FOR THE PRESIDENCY because I've seen proud men who wish only to work in dignity, but they cannot because their jobs are gone and no one — neither industry, labor, nor government — has cared enough to help.

We must begin to end this disgrace of this other America.

...

Even if we act to erase material poverty there is another great task. It is to confront the poverty of satisfaction — a lack of purpose and dignity — that inflicts us all. Too much and too long we seem to have surrendered community excellence and community values in the mere accumulation of material things.

Our GNP, now, is over $800 billion dollars a year, but that GNP — if we should judge America by that — that GNP counts air pollution and cigarette advertising, and ambulances to clean highways of carnage. It counts special locks for our doors and the jail for those who break them. It counts the destruction of our redwoods and the loss of our natural wonder in chaotic sprawl. It counts napalm and the cost of a nuclear war-head, and armored cars for police who fight riots in our streets . . . and the television programs, which glorify violence in order to sell toys to our children. Yet GNP does not allow for the health of our children, the quality of their education, or the joy of their play.

. . .

It measures neither our wit nor our courage, neither our wisdom nor our learning; neither our compassion nor our devotion to our country; it measures everything, in short, except that which makes life worthwhile. And it can tell us everything about America except why we are proud that we are Americans.

. . .

From the beginning our proudest boast was that we, here in this country, would be the best hope for all of mankind. And now, as we look at the war in Vietnam, we wonder if we still hold a decent respect for the opinions of mankind. And whether they have maintained a decent respect for us, or whether like Athens of old, we will forfeit sympathy and support, and ultimately security, in a single-minded pursuit of our own goals and our own objectives.

The Fieldhouse erupted. Everyone stamping their feet and chanting — they were one with the candidate. The crowd noise morphed into one loud pulsating mantra: "All the way with RFK! All the way with RFK!"

Slowly the candidate's traveling party disentangled themselves from an over-embracing KU crowd squishing in on them. Their adoration startled even Kennedy's most seasoned advance man, Jim Tolan, who, as they were departing, worried for the Senator's life.

Los Angeles Times Washington Bureau chief Robert Donovan wrote, "At times his speeches at Kansas State and the University of Kansas seemed to have a spellbinding effect on the students." Hearing the truth is a stunning experience. For some, it might take time for the message to sink in. Others get the message and responded instantly. The State of Kansas was a stunning first stop.

The first day of spring the Kennedy Campaign headed south of the Mason-Dixon Line, stopping at Vanderbilt University in Nashville, Tennessee. There RFK was to participate in the school's annual Freedom of Speech Symposium: IMPACT, the 1968 topic was The Destiny of Dissent. RFK titled his speech, "The Value of Dissent:"

> THOSE WHO NOW CALL for an end to dissent seem not to understand what this country is all about. For debate and dissent are the very heart of the American process. We have followed the wisdom of Greece: "All things are to be examined and brought into question. There is no limit set to thought." For debate is all we have to prevent past errors from leading us down the road to disaster. How else is error to be corrected, if not by the informed reason of dissent?
>
> ...
>
> Only broad and fundamental dissent will allow us to confront — not only material poverty — but the poverty of satisfaction that afflicts us all. So if we are uneasy about our country today, perhaps it is because . . . we know that our happiness will come not from the goods we have, but from the good we do together.
>
> ...
>
> Our country is in danger. Not just from foreign enemies; but above all from our own misguided policies and what they can do to this country. There is a con-

test, not for the rule of America, but for the heart of America.

...

I ask you, as tens of thousands of young men and women are doing all over this land, to organize yourselves, and then to go forth and work for new policies – work to change our direction – and thus restore our place at the point of moral leadership, in our country, in our own hearts, and all around the world.

Young Richard A. Coleman, one of many who shook the Senator's hand, remembered the moment, "When RFK spoke at Vanderbilt the sense of history was strong and people cheered wildly in support of almost everything he said." [University of Vanderbilt website - Richard A. Coleman, 2016]

The packed auditorium gave RFK a rousing standing ovation. Again, departing was total chaos. CBS commentator Roger Mudd told TV audiences that Nashville had become, "Mashville," as crushing crowds tried to reach out and touch Senator Robert Francis Kennedy of New York, a Catholic candidate for President.

RFK's return to the University of Alabama at Tuscaloosa later that afternoon was a crucial test of the support Kennedy would garner in the Deep South. His civil rights battle in 1963 with Governor Wallace loomed ominously over his return visit.

At Tuscaloosa's small airport, as RFK and Marine Colonel John Glenn's vehicle started to leave for the campus, Col. Glenn spotted a young boy hoisting a sign that read, "Bama Backs Bobby." Instantly Glenn had the boy inside the car meeting a bemused Senator Kennedy. [Univ. Alabama website - Elizabeth Holmes, Sept. 2016, "Comment."]

Before speaking at EMPHASIS '68, an annual student-financed symposium of ideas, RFK privately met with recent college graduate, James Hood, who in 1963 was one of the two students of African descent to enter the University of Alabama.

Foster Auditorium, where Governor George Wallace had
initially blocked entry in '63 to the two students, was filled to
capacity in 1968. Instead of emanating Southern hostility the
feeling was more of Southern hospitality. Astronaut Glenn, as
heroic an American figure as there was, proudly introduced the
Senator from New York who was, "Campaigning for the Presidency."

RFK described a politics of change that was aimed at mo-
bilizing citizen involvement to create a national consensus for
redirecting the country. To encompass everyone in this movement, Kennedy proposed, before an enthusiastic 'Bama crowd
of 9,000, the need for a dialogue about national reconciliation,
and the importance of the students' roles in catalyzing a spirit
of American renewal.

His speech was titled "America at The Crossroads."

THIS ELECTION will mean nothing if it leaves us, after it is all over, as divided as we were when it began.
We have to begin to put our country together again. So
I believe that any who seek high office this year must
go before all Americans: Not just those who agree with
them, but also those who disagree; recognizing that it is
not just our supporters, not just those who are for us, but
all Americans, who we must lead in the difficult years
ahead. And this is why I have come at the outset of my
campaign, not to New York or Chicago or Boston, but
here to Alabama.

...

Some have said there are many issues on which we disagree. For my part I do not believe these disagreements
are as great as the principles that unite us. And I also
think we can confront those issues with candor and
truth, and confront each other as men. We need not paper over our differences on specific issues — if we can,
as we must, remember always our common burden and
our common hope as Americans.

...

For history has placed us all — Northerner and South-
erner, black and white — within a common border and
under a common law. All of us, from the wealthiest and
most powerful of men, to the weakest and hungriest
of children, share one precious possession: The name
American.

So I come to Alabama to ask you to help in the task
of national reconciliation.

There may have been rednecks in the audience, but it was hard
to discern them amidst the exuberant crowd, who at the conclusion of his speech, showered RFK with their unqualified and
highly audible support.

Moody Connell, a member of the press, saw his speech from
a local perspective: "That Robert Kennedy could overcome the
anger once held due to the civil rights movement, and drew a
thunderous applause, demonstrates that Alabama was making
adjustments and was over-whelmed by JFK's assassination in
Dallas." [Univ. of Alabama website - Moody Connell, May 7, 2016, "Comment"]

Political reporter Jules Witcover felt that "once freed of a long
self-discipline against open criticism of Johnson, RFK became a
force on the stump seldom seen in American national politics."

19

VIVA KENNEDY

Energized by the over-the-top reception he received in Middle America during the first week of his campaign, Kennedy flew to the West Coast aboard a commercial flight filled with reporters, contributors, and staff. They landed in San Francisco to a tumultuous Bay Area reception described by Carl Greenberg of the *Los Angeles Times* as, "uproarious, shrieking, and frenzied."

In Monterey, as they boarded TWA to LAX, "an unmistakable gladness was in the air."

Robert Kennedy had begun his recovery from his brother's murder by taking steps he had never taken before. On March 24, 1965 he became the first to scale newly named Mt. Kennedy, a 13,944-foot peak in the Canadian Yukon, his first mountain climbing experience. His LAX arrival was exactly three years later . . . March 24, 1968. Now he was taking steps that were being followed by millions.

Youngest RFK Supporter at LAX 3/24/68 *Photo: Joel Siegel, UCLA KELP, and later ABC-TV's entertainment editor.*

I was living in West LA at the time, so I decided to check out the scene of Kennedy's arrival at TWA's terminal. There had been snippets in the news, but I wanted to see firsthand what his reception would be like. I drove my VW bug to LAX, and once parked I strapped my five-month-old son into a backpack, his head bobbing safely above my shoulders, a Kennedy pin affixed, front and center, to his hand-knit cap.

The waiting crowd of mainly women completely filled the low-ceilinged terminal hallways from wall to wall, literally a sea of happy and expectant people.

Upon RFK's arrival, the crowd surrounding me became electrified and surged to the point that I could no longer touch the floor or the walls. The mushrooming crowd lifted me up and I flowed out of the terminal in this sea of cheerful humanity as victorious shouts of "Viva Kennedy" echoed musically through the terminal's tiled hallways.

It was the only stampede I'd ever been in. It was frightening being out of control, but it was also exhilarating. No one was hurt. More importantly, we all witnessed the fact that the President's brother had indeed picked up the Torch. Change was coming like a hurricane. The Campaign for the Democratic Party's Nomination for President would be over in five months.

That night 6,000 supporters crammed into the Greek Theater's 4,500 seats, plus 3,000 more supporters camped outside the gates listening via portable speakers.

RFK was rolling through California like a surfer riding the crest of an unfolding wave. Crowds swarmed him at each stop: Sacramento, San Jose and now L.A. Everyone wanted to hear him. The aisles were filled with people and the night air was filled with high expectations.

At long last was the end to the vile Vietnam War in sight?

The moment Robert Kennedy walked on stage the audience went ballistic. Like at LAX, the crowd surged. Some might have seen the enthusiasm as hysteria, while others saw it as redemptive.

An answer to war's horrors?

They were not disappointed.

RFK admitted his campaign was in response to LBJ's failure of leadership; and he took off from there:

WE HAVE HAD PROBLEMS in the past. But at the same time we have shown that we can deal with our adversaries without bloodshed, as in the Cuban Missile Crisis.

We know that we can move toward protecting mankind from nuclear disaster, as with the . . . Limited Test Ban Treaty. We know we can reduce the tensions between black and white, not just through laws, but through personal leadership.

We know that this Nation can be fired by idealism and will serve the needs of others by peaceful means, as through the Peace Corps. Together, we can make this a nation where young people do not seek the false peace of drugs . . . . Together we can make this a nation where every citizen will have an equal chance at dignity and decency. Together, Americans are the most decent, generous and compassionate people in the world. Divided they are collections of islands . . . something has happened to that guiding spirit.

All the phrases which have meant so much to Americans — peace and progress, justice and compassion, leadership and idealism — often sound not like stirring reminders of our nation, but call forth the cynical laughter or hostility of our young and many of our adults. Not because they do not believe them, but because they do not think our leaders mean them. These specific failures reflect the larger failure of national purpose. We do not know where we are going. We have been stripped of goals and values and direction, as we move aimlessly and rather futilely from crisis to crisis and danger to danger. And the record shows that kind of approach will not only not solve problems, it will only deepen them.

This is not simply the result of bad policies and lack of skill. It flows from the fact that for almost the first time the national leadership is calling upon the darker impulses of the American spirit — not, perhaps, deliberately, but through its action and the example it sets — an example where integrity, truth, honor, and all the rest seem like words to fill out speeches rather than guiding beliefs . . . .

The issue in this election, therefore, is whether this new and startling path shall continue into the future, or whether we shall turn back to our roots and to our traditions so that future historians shall view this period as the great aberration of American history. That is the issue you must decide this year. That is why I am running . . ..

I hope to offer you a way in which the people themselves can lead the way back to those ideals which are the source of national strength and generosity and compassion of deed.

The battle was on. LBJ had been thrown under the bus. America's failure of leadership was "all the President's fault." Every able-bodied soldier had to step up.

After a year of creating and administrating UCLA Extension educational programs for business people, I had mastered the intricacies of my job. I was, in fact, ahead of the game in that I had my three-day short courses (The Art of Franchising and AFSC-375 Systems Management for military contracting) already organized and advertised. My week-long conference: The Idea Institute, my most expensive offering designed for top management, was set for April 8–11 on campus at the GBA building. It featured heavyweight thinkers and doers exploring radical art (Professor Kurt von Meier) to ads (Mel Blanc), from math (Professor Edward Thorp's card-counting probability theory) to media (Professor Edmund Carpenter, Marshall McLuhan's decade-long associate at University of Toronto).

Publicity for these top-tier offerings had been included in the upcoming UCLA Extension Catalogue. Select mailing lists would receive a fancy brochure produced by Extension's art department to sell the class offerings; conferences and short courses required brochures.

University Extension programs had to pay for themselves. A minimum number of students had to sign up for a class or it was canceled. There was no money in the state's education master plan for adult education, only statewide officials were in the budget. UCLA Extension was in the business of selling adult education and had developed a nationwide reputation in cutting a profit.

My "Voter Information Program" series of one-day conferences was scheduled to examine a Mass Transit proposal on the November ballot that would run down Wilshire Boulevard to the beach; even so, educating people about Mass Transit was a gamble in car-centric Los Angeles.

At this moment in time, I was essentially free to get involved in the Kennedy Campaign every afternoon and evening.

Curious, I went to Kennedy Campaign Headquarters at 5615 Wilshire Blvd., an enormous, two-story block-long Spanish Colonial Revival edifice built in 1928. The tenant, the family-owned Ralphs Markets, had just been sold to Federated Department Stores and the mammoth building was empty.

I was stunned by the number of people pouring into the building seeking involvement in Robert Kennedy's campaign and there was nothing for them to do besides registering to vote.

Every type of person was coming through the door — white, Black, rich, poor, Mexican, Asian, blue-collar, white-collar, housewives, students, seniors . . . even movie stars.

In front of the long white stone building with its red roof tiles, soaking up the sunlight, I connected with the young civil rights organizer, John Lewis, past Chairman of SNCC (Student Non-Violent Coordinating Committee), who had just arrived from Atlanta. He was onboard.

Everyone from everywhere was stepping up.

This was a national campaign to recapture the government and redirect our collective efforts toward a "strategy of peace."

Thanks to my community organizing experiences in the Peace Corps, I decided to create a volunteer group to corral these people walking into headquarters and to urge them to organize a

Kennedy Coffee Klatch at their home to discuss Robert Kennedy's newly published book, *To Seek A Newer World*.

Being an unknown, I asked the Olympian Rafer Johnson, former UCLA Student Body President and also a member of the KELPS, to be Co-Chairman of the Young Professionals for Kennedy, using his name recognition and my sweat to get people meaningfully involved in the campaign. I then printed stationery and volunteer cards, finagled two desks, a chair, a blackboard on wheels, and started signing up young professionals for Kennedy at the campaign headquarters.

Full-time workers were distinct from students, although older graduate students felt more comfortable with us Young Professionals. We were soon organizing Kennedy Coffee Klatches all over Los Angeles County, supplying paperbacks of RFK's new book, bumper stickers, pins, and voter registration forms. If a Klatch had a dozen people confirmed, the Young Professionals would send a speaker; the more guests confirmed the more recognizable the speaker's reputation. Celebrity speaker requests were funneled to Frank Mankiewicz's desk.

Frank's office was on the mezzanine, where a series of offices encircled a wide-open ground floor that rose straight up a 40-foot-wide, 60-foot-tall tower. This gigantic indoor space was in the west end of the Ralph's building and magically muffled the ground floor noise.

Frank was no longer on the road and had delegated most of his press responsibilities. He had become an on-site campaign strategist. Winning California was essential to winning the Democratic Party nomination for President. As a WWII vet, Frank had become a hard-boiled realist who had underlying philosophies supporting his operational objectives. He was a newsman, had a Columbia University M.A in journalism, and was an attorney, with a degree from UC Berkeley Boalt Hall School of Law. He had been a candidate for State Assemblyman on L.A.'s wealthy Westside.

Frank knew the players and the power brokers. Entertainment celebrities from filmmaker Warren Beatty to *Laugh-In's*

Goldie Hawn lined up outside his office to offer their services.

The Mankiewicz brothers, Joseph and Herman (who was Frank's father), were authentic Hollywood royalty. Over the decades they had earned the respect of the film community and of Beverly Hills film financiers by making colossal Academy Award-winning movies like *Citizen Kane*, *All About Eve*, *A Letter to Three Wives*, *Guys & Dolls*, and *Cleopatra*.

Frank, eldest of the next generation, was the embodiment of the Mankiewicz family's front line commitment to social justice; movies and the media were secondary. His activism on behalf of migratory workers in 1960 had brought him to the attention of Presidential candidate U.S. Senator John F. Kennedy.

Professor Guzmán wrote again to Mankiewicz, "Please make certain that I and other Chicanos are not left out. We have a hell of a lot of young Chicano power that identifies with the Senator . . . . We need Senator Robert F. Kennedy and he needs us."

Not surprisingly, Professor Guzmán was named to California's Presidential Delegation committed to Kennedy along with César Chavez, Bert Corona, Honorable Mervyn Dymally, Willard Murray, Paul Schrade, Rafer Johnson, Victor Palmieri, and William Norris.

The Kennedy Campaign was the spark that activists had been waiting for. César Chávez and veteran union organizer Humberto "Bert" Corona, Director of MAPA, invited Alberto Juárez, UMAS chair of 25 chapters, to join Viva Kennedy, which Alberto did.

Working with Bert Corona was a no-brainer for Alberto who, like Bert, had Mexican revolutionary blood in his veins — Alberto's great-uncle had been a general in Pancho Villa's army of the 1910 Mexican Revolution. Being a staunch supporter of *la comunidad* (the community) was in-bred in both men.

Alberto considered Bert a model of the responsible citizen, a pragmatic leader, and a prime example of one person's self-sacrifice for la comunidad. He believed Bert was a great role model, "He was intelligent, educated, and fair-minded."

Like Bert, Alberto could see the long arc of history, "To be part of the Kennedy legacy, running on a national progressive agenda, was good enough to take on its face. It was a trifecta of opportunities: to learn, to play a part in history, and to be a part of the future."

Still, going against his UMAS colleagues was not an easy choice for Alberto, his wife and their emerging family.

On the other hand, I was a community college transfer in my first year at UCLA; I had a job with L.A. County Probation Department working midnights as a Group Supervisor in El Monte. The world exploding around me — from Delano to East L.A. — actually made the decision to join the Viva Kennedy Campaign simple. Now was the time for action.

Up and down the state of California we went. Bert took me to places I didn't know existed. We never bought food. Wherever we went, the people fed us. It was a wildly creative period. I even designed a "*Viva* Kennedy" pin.

20

UNITING DISPARATE ELEMENTS

On campuses organizational chaos followed for the United Mexican American Students. "Betrayal" yelled a few militants.

But to most activists, the Kennedy Presidential Campaign and Latino demands from Central California to East L.A. were intertwined. Whether they saw themselves as Chicanos, or Mexican-Americans, or Hispanics, their futures were very much wrapped up in the success of RFK's national campaign for social justice and economic reform.

This was with the exception of Kennedy's opposition to the Vietnam War. It was a sensitive subject at odds with the traditional patriotic image of Mexican American warriors.

As a Vietnam-era vet, Alberto Juárez thought the influence of Guzmán's research on Vietnam fatalities of Spanish-surnamed soldiers in five Southwestern states was the tipping point: "Guzmán provided statistical evidence for something we intuitively felt. His work gave us the ammunition we needed to turn the tide — a very important element."

As a WWII veteran, Guzmán appealed to several UMAS leaders . . . veterans looking to make change. In Alberto's opinion:

Guzmán was the first person to give us any credibility. He held court for us young guys, while courting us to become activists. He was not only an accomplished neighborhood organizer, he was our first intellectual — he conducted a national study, cutting-edge research, and was an advocate of Brown Power. Ralph pulled no punches. In an article he wrote in late '68 about "Young Revolutionaries," he played cultural hardball, "The young militants are forcing Mexican-Americans to look squarely at themselves and to acknowledge their Indian ancestry. Most Mexicans don't want to."

Today's historians hardly mention Dr. Ralph C. Guzmán, UC-LA's first professor of Chicano Studies.

Nick Juárez, Ralph's lifelong friend and UCLA colleague, was with him throughout the Sixties, and until Guzmán's untimely death in 1985 at age 60, while he was serving as Provost of Merrill College at UC Santa Cruz. Thinking back, Nick agreed that the March-June scene of '68 was "murky" with cultural identity choices and a rapidly growing militancy: "Ralph was an old school organizer, building a cadre one by one. He pushed me to do things I didn't want to do. His training for conducting interviews for MASP was precise: 'pay attention to the client being interviewed. Be nice to the children. All parents like to hear praise for their children.'"

Eventually, Nick closed down the MASP fieldwork, and Ralph sent him to research migrant worker housing for the State of California. Then he was sent to teach at Belvedere Jr. High to see how they were treating the students; Ralph hoped Nick would gather enough evidence for an exposé. And much against his wishes, Ralph thought Nick should join Albuquerque-based Jobs for Progress' Operation SER (Service-Employment-Redevelopment), funded by OEO and Department of Labor, as their national research director.

Shortly after managing the $100M project, 30-year-old Nick started his own management consulting business in 1969, Juárez & Associates, and began promoting peaceful change here and abroad — empowering people, non-governmental organizations, and governments with market research and data analysis, in Spanish or English.

Nick's recollection of Dr. Guzman rings with praise:

RALPH WAS NOT a militant. He believed you could change things from the inside. All his life he had done it. I followed Ralph's example to do something 'long-lasting and consequential;' and I'm still at it 50 years later. Dr. Ralph C. Guzmán was tenacious, transparent, and factual, which is why he became Deputy Assistant Secretary of State for Latin America. Not bad for an immigrant kid from Moroleon, Mexico, growing up during the Depression in East L.A. before WWII. Ralph saw it all. Did it all. Ironically, the uninformed militancy of the day drowned out the memory of perhaps America's greatest Chicano activist-intellectual. He is an unsung hero of our cultural revolution that is still on-going.

With the uniting of the disparate elements of the Mexican American movements behind RFK, and in the wake of RFK's Greek Theater speech, LBJ surprisingly withdrew his bid for re-election on March 31st 1968. The world of American politics exploded again.

Two weeks of RFK's Campaign and ka-BOOM — the President was down and out! Hubert Humphrey, his Vice President, would run as his surrogate, abide by LBJ's policies and offer no repudiation of The War, thereby sabotaging his own liberal credentials. Was it the Greek Theater speech that LBJ never wanted to hear again that prompted him to pull out?

Clearly Eugene McCarthy did not faze LBJ, but RFK did. His broad support among minorities and the downtrodden would make his run for the Presidency unstoppable. LBJ knew that and bailed.

On April 4th 1967 Martin Luther King Jr. gave his famous "Beyond Vietnam" speech where he dramatically broke with LBJ and called for an end to the Vietnam War. Exactly one year later to the day, Dr. King was assassinated in broad daylight.

Not knowing what had happened, I was in South Central delivering boxes of voter registration forms to Willard Murray, an aide to State Senator Dymally. When I arrived at his 77th Street office late in the day, he told me that I didn't need to stay, and that I should actually leave "Immediately. South Central is blowin'," he growled, "Martin Luther King was murdered today in Memphis."

As I drove north toward downtown Los Angeles, from the elevated segment of the Harbor Freeway (Interstate 110) I could see fires erupting across the South Central landscape. I was not afraid, but I was deeply saddened by the sudden turn of events and the precipitous twisting of emotions. One week LBJ's gone, Hooray; the next week we lose Martin Luther King Jr., utter despair. It was unbelievable what Africa's slave descendants in America were forced to go through. Reverend King had made peace his number one objective and he was murdered. Black Power advocates who had called for violence would find greater reception of their goals now that the spokesman for non-violence — the 1964 Nobel Peace Prize Winner — had been assassinated for advocating peace.

Meanwhile, Robert Kennedy, with no police escort, drove to a neighborhood park in an impoverished section of Indianapolis, Indiana where he had been scheduled to speak. A makeshift podium was placed on the rear of a flatbed truck. Extemporaneously Senator Kennedy acted the peacemaker and announced to an unsuspecting crowd the murder of Martin Luther King, Jr. For the first time, he spoke in public about his brother being killed by a white man. Turning his cheek, he offered his antidote to revenge and violence:

> WHAT WE NEED in the United States is not division; what we need in the United States is not hatred; what we need in the United States is not violence and lawlessness, but is love, and wisdom, and compassion toward one another, and a feeling of justice toward those who still suffer within our country, whether they be white or whether they be black.

The crowd wept, applauded, and went home silently in the dark.

That evening and far into the next morning at the stately Marott Hotel, Indianapolis' first luxury hotel, RFK and his aides worked feverishly over a more thoughtful and more nuanced response to Reverend King's murder, collecting input from Ted Sorenson in D.C., and from Mankiewicz and Walinsky.

The next morning, en route to Cleveland, RFK revised his speech. He was to speak at a luncheon for Cleveland's distinguished City Club at the Sheraton-Cleveland Hotel. Twenty-two hundred citizens had paid to hear Robert Kennedy; two local television stations had cut away from the King Memorial coverage to broadcast his speech live. The wealthy, primarily white, audience of Cleveland wanted to hear what Robert Kennedy had to say in this time of national crisis.

To a tense but courteous audience he delivered his message "On the Mindless Menace of Violence:"

THIS IS A TIME of shame and sorrow. It is not a day for politics. I have saved this one opportunity to speak briefly to you about this mindless menace of violence in America, which again stains our land and every one of our lives.

. . .

What has violence ever accomplished? What has it ever created? No martyr's cause has ever been stilled by his assassin's bullet. No wrongs have ever been righted by riots and civil disorders. A sniper is only a coward, not a hero, and an uncontrolled, uncontrollable mob is only the voice of madness, not the voice of the people.

. . .

For there is another kind of violence, slower, but just as deadly destructive as the shot, or the bomb in the night. This is the violence of institutions, indifference and inaction and slow decay. This is the violence that afflicts the poor, that poisons relations between men because their skin has different colors. This is a slow destruction of a child by hunger, and schools without books and homes without heat in the winter. This is the breaking of a man's spirit by denying him the chance to stand as a father and as a man among other men. And this too afflicts us all.

. . .

Our lives on this planet are too short and the work to be done too great to let this spirit flourish any longer in our land. Of course we cannot vanish it with a program, nor with a resolution. But we can perhaps remember — even if only for a time — that those who live with us are our brothers, that they share with us the same short moment of life, that they seek — as do we — nothing but the chance to live out their lives in purpose and happiness, winning what satisfaction and fulfillment they can. Surely this bond of common faith, this bond of common goal, can begin to teach us something. Surely we can learn, at least, to look at those around us as fellow men and surely we can begin to work a little harder to bind up the wounds among us and to become in our hearts brothers and countrymen once again.

Kennedy's speech lasted ten minutes.

The audience, shattered by the simplicity of his message, its poetic essence, gave him a standing ovation. Against tradition, he took no questions and left immediately for D.C., suspending his Presidential campaign until MLK's funeral proceedings had concluded.

He provided a charter jet for Coretta Scott's use in picking up Dr. King's body in Memphis and returning it to Atlanta. He had AT&T install extra phone lines at King's home and a bank of phones installed at his church. RFK then waited at home in Hickory Hill for instructions from Dr. King's widow, Coretta Scott.

King's murder affected everyone from coast to coast. The horror of political assassinations arose, again, in our land of the free. Since there weren't enough ballots to stop the Peace Movement, bullets would be used. The message was clear. The timing was telling. The status quo was not changing. Hawks were intent on polarizing the public discourse over the Vietnam War, metaphorically yelling, "To Hell with the Bill of Rights!"

At the same time, as if mirroring this turmoil, *Catch My Soul*, a musical adaptation of William Shakespeare's *Othello* had opened at the new Ahmanson Theater in downtown L.A.

In an effort to escape the madness after MLK's murder, we were the first in line to buy tickets.

The show featured legendary Rock & Roller Jerry Lee Lewis ("Whole Lotta Shakin' Goin' On," "Great Balls of Fire") as Iago, wearing, in one scene, a full-body, backless Red Devil costume complete with a long red pointed tail. Seeing Jerry Lee standing at his green and gold piano pounding out his legendary country R & B rhythms, and singing in a Shakespearean banter with saxophones blaring from the Elizabethan balconies that hung over the Ahmanson's broad stage, was a mind-blowing affair. Jaunty Jerry Lee stole the show.

Night after night the entertainment community lined up outside his stage door showering him with praise. "The Killer" had arrived and spectacularly taken L.A. with his Southern charm and prodigious talent as thoroughly as Sherman had taken Atlanta. Jerry Lee's evil Iago, playing opposite William Marshall's hesitant Othello, entangles and entraps the Moor who is lost in his blind affection for the very blond Desdemona. Jack Good's musical contained more in-your-face social issues than a Students for a Democratic Society (SDS) platform. Iago's treachery seemed the order of the day. Jerry Lee Lewis' devilish Iago was only a six-week treat for Los Angeles audiences: March 4th–April 13th, but his portrayal left me an image of betrayal that has lasted a lifetime. Shakespeare suddenly seemed accessible to my blue-collar trained brain.

A national coalition composed of all elements of society had to be mobilized to demonstrate to the political bosses that RFK could take the Democratic Party all the way. Kennedy would campaign in Indiana employing the "all-Americans" strategy, albeit high-risk, of simultaneously merging opposite interests and then representing them both.

The best expression of this daring coalition materialized April 15th in Gary, Indiana, a contentious steel mill town whose blue-collar workers claimed both European and African origins. Driving in an open convertible through the center of town with hometown boxing legend Tony Zale seated on one side and Mayor Richard Hatcher, the state's first African-American mayor, seated on the other side, RFK illustrated his enormous powers of persuasion, both actual and symbolic. The three of them rode to the white section of Gary and to the black section.

RFK, according to journalist Jack Newfield who was there, gave the same message to both communities: "Jobs are better than welfare; welfare creates dependency and work confers self-respect . . . we have to be tough on crime; riots are no solution to the problems." Each community, Newfield reported, responded enthusiastically to his message. RFK had tapped into the American ethos. When the working-class knows, there are no excuses for the elite not to know.

Returning to Indiana for a final 16-day 16-city stint leading up to the May 7th Primary, candidate Kennedy began at the University of Indiana's Medical School, the Nation's largest.

At Emerson Hall he spoke to 500 medical students, and delivered a blistering attack on the inequity of draft deferments granted for medical school students, but not for gas station attendants. "It is discriminatory," RFK argued. "Black soldiers deaths in Vietnam are more than twice their percent of the population."

RFK was authentic and straightforward. Even if you didn't champion his causes, his passion for them was inspiring. A questioner pithily asked, "Where are you going to get the money to pay for the programs you propose?"

The Senator's tart retort, "From you."

RFK with Children of Indiana. circa April 1968. *Unknown photographer. Gift, Jules Glazer, CA Campaign accountant.*

The last week of April, the Kennedy family and staff boarded an Election Train Special that traveled the same route as the famed Wabash Express. Whenever they stopped, an on-board banjo troop jumped up and played, "The Wabash Cannonball." It was in that folksy manner the Kennedys toured through Central Indiana, a casual meet and greet from the rear car's platform. Bobby's frank demeanor and self-effacing wit played well in rural America. He believed in the power of work. The ability to work with your hands, to build your home, these were values he held in common with conservative-minded Hoosiers, not to mention their dry wit. In Wabash, reputed light bulb capital of the world, handmade signs reflected local support, "Socket to 'em, Bobby."

On April 24th at Indiana University's Memorial Auditorium in Bloomington, RFK delivered his Foreign Policy plans and openly explored: "What we learned from Vietnam." He put forth so deft an argument on how to prevent the U.S. becoming involved in future Vietnams he swayed important political writers with his commonsense logic:

W E MUST ALSO KEEP this entire issue in its proper perspective. For whatever American interests are involved in the internal affairs of the Third World, they are very slight compared to the substantial threats, which potentially lie ahead. These have not been conquered by Vietnam; indeed, in many respects, it has made them far worse.

...

For the fourth danger is here at home. It is the danger that absorption in the problems of others will cause us to neglect the wealth and quality of our society. We cannot continue to deny and postpone the demands of our own people while spending billions in the name of the freedom of others. No nation can exert greater power of influence in the world than it can exercise over the streets of its own capital. A nation torn by injustice and violence, its streets patrolled by army units — if this is to be our country, we can doubt how long others will look to us for leadership, or seek our participation in their common ventures. America was a great force in the world, with immense prestige, long before we became a great military power. That power has come to us and we cannot renounce it, but neither can we afford to forget that the real constructive force in the world comes not from bombs, but from imaginative ideas, warm sympathies, and a generous spirit. These are qualities that cannot be manufactured by specialists in public relations. They are the natural qualities of a people pursuing decency and human dignity in its own undertakings without arrogance of hostility or delusions of superiority toward others; a people whose ideal for others are firmly rooted in the realities of the society we have built for ourselves.

The crowd of 4,000 interrupted his speech with loud applause 16 times. Crooner Bobby Darin nailed it: "Kennedy is the remedy," reported a *LIFE Magazine* photo caption.

On May 7th farmers, students, and steel workers of Polish and African origins sided with RFK. Even white voters of Gary who had supported George Wallace's run for President in 1964, switched. Indiana's Democratic Governor Roger Branigin was soundly defeated 42% to 31%; Senator Eugene McCarthy finished last.

The UAW's National Convention in Atlantic City, New Jersey on May 10th showcased Democratic candidates Humphrey and RFK, as well as the UAW's peerless example of supporting the poorest of workers, the NFW.

Dolores Huerta, a veteran organizer, born in northern New Mexico, and raised in Stockton, California, was now a national figure. She had delivered Delano's grape strike to the streets of Manhattan and made the grape boycott national. She thanked the UAW and its 3,000 delegates (representing 1.6 million workers) for their support and urged members to become involved in the grape boycott in their local communities.

(In 1970, after a five-year long boycott of table grapes, Dolores Huerta, NFW's lead negotiator, won a three-year-long contract with the entire California table grape industry, a monumental victory for agricultural workers.)

RFK, in his first speech since winning Indiana, as well as the District of Colombia, embraced the theme of peace, famously arguing, "U.S. cannot be the world's policeman. That is the lesson of Vietnam." He was adamant, "This nation must adopt a foreign policy which says, clearly and distinctly, no more Vietnams." The reason was obvious, "We cannot deny and postpone the demands of our own people, while spending billions in the name of freedom of others in nations around the world."

May 14th was the Nebraska Primary and Kennedy visited the state five times; McCarthy came but once. RFK's audience of 14,000 at the University of Nebraska in Omaha was the largest crowd in Nebraska's political history. Kennedy's key constituencies: the poor and the minorities were not in the mix; yet he did well in cashing in his Indiana bona fides. Kennedy's style of addressing problems in a straightforward manner and his self-deprecating style resonated with like-minded Midwesterners. He was not rushed and they were not rushing him. Surrounded by Ethel and his children he was seen more as a concerned family man than as a ruthless campaign manager. RFK's 51%–31% trouncing of McCarthy in Nebraska was therefore not surprising.

Kansas, Tennessee, and Alabama were no low-hanging gifts. Kennedy rolled the dice and told it like it was and those who saw the same reality responded. This was not just an anti-war movement. It was a movement dedicated to societal change: re-affirming old values while recalibrating public resource allocations in a more egalitarian fashion. If Heartland voters, some of our Nation's most conservative folks, approved of RFK, there was no stopping his return to the White House. RFK's focus on the problems and the aspirations of the everyday citizen appealed to Nebraskans; and the fact that Eugene McCarthy was the "First to challenge President Johnson" wasn't compelling enough of a reason to win their vote. The entire Nation was worried over the out-of-control war that We, The People, were being forced to finance.

Kennedy's strategy was to ask voters for their involvement in stopping the war. He wasn't saying, I'll be your General and lead you. He was saying that we are all needed in the effort to re-direct the Nation. His urging them to become involved was another permutation of his brother's Inaugural challenge: "Ask what you can do for your country." It was the classic battle over governance: the community-runs-the-government vs. the elite-will-do-it-for-you, minus a percentage for their troubles.

21

CAMPAIGN '68 — RFK HEADQUARTERS

Back in Los Angeles, no one at Hauser and Wilshire had to be told that RFK's conquering of the Heartland meant that in November there would finally be a government beholden to The People. Everyone knew. It felt like we were catching an enormous ocean-sized wave comprised of people, ideas, and dreams, a national wave that was rising up and transforming itself from a purveyor of war to a promoter of peace. We had our work cut out for us. Fortuitously, I was at ground zero. I was going to ride this wave all the way to November and beyond. Restoring the New Frontier was now a reality. Finally, after the nightmare of 11/22/63, there was a way back to world peace and justice for all.

Selling Dictaphones for a commission and switching boxcars for the Santa Fe had not been satisfying. They were expediencies to suffer through while you figured out where in society the honorable work was to be found, where, together, we could do even better. Creating adult education programs was a step up and in the right direction but limited in its impact and its focus was too broad. With the nation hemorrhaging and with only one life to live, I was going all in with RFK.

The Young Professionals for Kennedy tables became a magnet for volunteers walking in the front doors. It operated as a hub for providing campaign supplies and for filling speaker requests to countless Kennedy Coffee Klatches: who's in charge, how many coming, where's the location, what time? The Coordinating Committee had grown to over a dozen activists who daily manned the Young Professionals operation. People I didn't know manned the tables and were busy doing what was needed. Joy Thornton, John Basson, Booker Griffin joined the effort on a daily basis, so I added their names to the stationery. This was an all-inclusive organizing effort. Young professionals — social workers, teachers, nurses, lawyers, bookkeepers, engineers — carried paperbacks and voter registration forms every evening to coffee klatches. Young Professionals spoke in every neighborhood of L.A. County, except for possibly San Marino.

Unbelievably, Frank Mankiewicz's secretary, Lucy, had been — 12 years before — the head cheerleader at my high school in San Berdoo! She had been a year ahead of me, which had not stopped me from trying to impress Miss Lucy.

Now, Lucy was at Ground Zero of RFK's Presidential Campaign. I couldn't imagine how she, a rah-rah girl from Berdoo, had become Frank's right arm, although her physical appearance and style of clothing had dramatically changed since I last saw her in 1956. At first I didn't even recognize her when she called out to me.

Her long, brown, shoulder-length hair and hatchet bangs had replaced a hair-sprayed bouffant. Instead of wearing a crisp, cotton Lanz dress with applied rickrack trim, she now wore a suede vest and a long-sleeved turtleneck, a hip-hugging short skirt and knee-length socks. Lucy was now a fox.

Occasionally, Lucy would pass messages to me from Frank, like, "Arrange to pick up the Kennedy children at LAX."

I was told there were six children. I was too busy to go, scheduling Kennedy Coffee Klatches.

The Kennedy children were delivered without incident to the Beverly Hills Hotel & Bungalows, transported by two total strangers: my wife and Marc Horowitz, a UCLA classmate who owned a three-seat station wagon.

For most families, the idea of strangers picking up their children at the airport is asking for trouble. For the campaigning Kennedys, their supporters were extended family. There was never any negativity at headquarters. The campaign staff and its growing army of volunteers were all happy campers. We were advancing a product that more and more people wanted. The masses normally ignore the two-party shuffle (hence 45% of the public don't vote in national elections; local turnouts are even embarrassingly lower). With RFK, they had found a prospect they believed would lead our nation to peace and justice, even for our most vulnerable citizens. Everyone wanted to help and everyone's involvement was welcomed.

Since it was obvious Kennedy was going the whole distance, I decided to get more campaign experience in order to be of more value in the final push following the August Democratic Nominating Convention in Chicago.

Lucy connected me with "Advance" and they added me to the May 20th Temple Isaiah stop. That morning, before they picked up the Senator, I met the Advance team's car parked in front of Temple Isaiah at 10345 West Pico Boulevard; it would be the last stop of the day.

The trunk of their car was filled with pressed white shirts, ties, boxes of cuff links, and tie clasps. When I asked why so much? Tolan, head of Advance, replied, "They rip the clothes right off his back."

Tolan gave me my instructions: "He's scheduled to speak around 6 pm. Get here an hour earlier to help with crowd control."

The Senator's Campaign team toured South Central, Long Beach, flew to San Diego, flew back to Pomona and motored west toward East L. A. where, at a campaign stop in the Montebello crowd, an enterprising young man in the crowd stole the Senator's shoes right off his feet, both of them.

Around 6 pm, Mankiewicz showed up at Temple Isaiah. Frank was not with the Senator. Apparently the candidate and his team were running so late that Frank came over from headquarters to entertain the waiting audience.

I did not know that Kennedy's speech was to be about Israel, the Middle East, and the Nuclear Arms Race. Kennedy was in favor of a Nuclear Weapons Freeze and hoped the Russians would follow suit. RFK was also in favor of selling Phantom Fighter jets to Israel should the Russians decline.

Everyone at the Temple was Jewish, mostly from the congregation, and like most of the men there Frank was wearing a yarmulke. I was such a blue-collar bumpkin I didn't realize he was Jewish.

Growing up in blue-collar Berdoo, I only had one Jewish high school classmate, a neighbor named Glasscock, who I lost contact with after he changed his name. His older brother, Richard, didn't, and for years he ran UCLA Medical School's Department of Urology.

For two hours Frank Mankiewicz entertained the waiting crowd with his behind-the-scenes stories about Hollywood, Israel, prospects for ending the War, day-to-day difficulties of conducting a Presidential campaign, and the all-important balancing of Hollywood's temperamental personalities. It was a semi-hilarious discussion of serious matters, an intellectual game of comic one-upsmanship, the likes of which I'd never seen in stolid Berdoo.

Around 8:30 pm Senator Kennedy arrived. He was exhausted. Actually he looked dazed. Before entering Temple Isaiah he borrowed campaign aide Fred Dutton's shoes and wore them as he flatly walked through his Israel-Arms speech. I was shocked at how mechanical he seemed.

At the close of his speech Frank asked the crowd of 600 if there were any questions. Instantly, RFK came to life, as if he had been in diapause waiting for this singular moment to emerge. He sparkled in his defense of a nuclear weapons test ban; he chided a student questioner for taking a deferment while poor blacks took his place on the frontlines of Vietnam. Clearly, Kennedy was invigorated by the spontaneous exchange. The intellectual effort to convert difficult questions into positive responses appeared to be his favorite mind game.

While no one knew it at the time, young Stephen Saltzman of the Temple Isaiah congregation, who later became a Deputy Mayor during Tom Bradley's five-term 20-year-long Administration, brought a Mannlicher-Carcano rifle with him — the same type used to kill JFK. Similarly, he purchased the rifle through the mail for $19.95 and bought ammunition at a local gun shop on Hollywood Boulevard, for a class project at Pierce Community College. Saltzman was proving how easy it was to bring a gun to a public event. His gun control thesis concluded, "No change in gun control since 1963." He left the gun and bullets in the trunk of his car that night.

Logically, you couldn't deny that reality. You just didn't think about it in hopes that all the positive energy RFK was generating would somehow protect him. Los Angeles Mayor Sam Yorty had expressly ordered the LAPD not to provide security for U.S. Senator Robert Kennedy's visit. This lack of security was an invitation to madness all but a few ignored.

The May 24th SRO (Standing Room Only) fund-raising concert at the L.A. Sports Arena featured The Byrds and a host of celebrities: "Angie Dickinson, Carol Channing, Shirley MacLaine, Gene Barry, Gene Kelly, Andy Williams, Henry Mancini, Alan King, Jerry Lewis, Sonny & Cher, Mahalia Jackson, Roosevelt Grier and many more," said the flyer.

Attending the celebrity-laced concert sent campaign volunteers, including Young Professionals, scurrying about in search of tickets. As the prospects for RFK's victory grew, so grew the desire by the young lawyers to be in charge of the Young Professionals, a non-incorporated group that had no bank account but one they assumed would soon be recognized for its meritorious activities. "According to Robert's Rules of Order," droned one of L.A. City's newest prosecutors, a Harvard law graduate, "there should be a meeting to elect officers."

On May 28th Kennedy lost the Oregon Democratic Primary to McCarthy. While there are several theories as to why, RFK's diagnosis was succinct, "I do best where people are hurting." Oregonians were proud of its independent persona, of being the first state whose U.S. Senator, Wayne Morris, voted against the War. That "independent" image might also explain the absence of any racial minorities living in lily-white lumber-jacked Oregon.

Kennedy might even have won had not Drew Pearson's national newspaper column four days before the election scandalously revealed that, as Attorney General, RFK had approved the FBI's wiretap of Martin Luther King Jr.

The media discussions, back and forth over the difference between a wiretap and a bug, kept many Oregon fence sitters at home on Election Day. One thing Pearson's column unequivocally illustrated was that FBI Director J. Edgar Hoover was still a Kennedy family nemesis.

Despite RFK's loss to McCarthy in Oregon, I did not see McCarthy beating Kennedy in California, not even coming close. United Auto Workers and the Teamsters were on board; César Chávez's National Farm Workers, Ted Watkins' Watts Up, Tom Watson of IBM and Harold Williams of Hunts Foods — all of them — were on board. The grass roots were so widely spread out they were in communities where citizens had never before registered to vote.

Bill Norris called; he needed someone to come downtown to pick up and deliver an important package to the Wilshire Blvd. Headquarters. My old Peace Corps pal D.J. Boyd and his deceptively youthful appearance was the perfect candidate. "It was $10,000 cash," the former coalminer's son remarked decades later, "The Kennedy campaign had lots of money," the retired federal judge laughingly recalled, "It takes a lot of green energy to get out the vote. Poor people normally don't have babysitters or transportation; catching a cab to the polls in South Central is asking for the miraculous."

The demand for celebrity speakers was coming from all parts of Southern California. Pre-election parties and discussion groups to decide whether to vote for McCarthy or Kennedy had mushroomed throughout the Southland. A Kennedy Klatch on the Venice-Del Rey peninsula demanded "a Kennedy family member to speak at their party of 50 to 60."

The host, a brash Venice real estate speculator, was angry that his wish wasn't going to be granted, and, in retaliation, he invited the Eugene McCarthy campaign to send their speakers to his margarita-fueled Klatch. His guests were not kids but grown-ups with checkbooks, and who were already registered to vote.

Besides hosting a Coffee Klatch at my Westwood duplex, I had never been to another one because I was so busy organizing them, but this particular Thursday night affair at the beach peaked my curiosity. In the two-month effort by the Young Professionals to organize hundreds and hundreds of Kennedy Coffee Klatches throughout L.A. County here was the only person who acted like a jerk.

I was not the only one sucked in by this man's obnoxiousness; Mankiewicz also showed up. So did film actress Myrna Loy, a McCarthy supporter; she was Venice High School's most famous graduate and, officially, "America's Film Sweetheart."

After the campaign discussion was over and the party was breaking up, I listened to Frank and Myrna talking while seated at a dinette table in the developer's kitchen. Several other guests listened in as Hollywood Royalty chatted right before our eyes. What they discussed had nothing to do with the campaign. They were talking about the good old days of movie-making, movies made after WWII ended in 1945 up through 1948.

"Best movies ever made," Myrna asserted softly. Frank nodded his head knowingly, and they then began reciting to each other their favorites: *Spellbound* (1945), *Mildred Pierce* (1945), *The Lost Weekend* (1945), *Razor's Edge* (1946), *Postman Always Rings Twice* (1946), *Best Years of Our Lives* (1946), *Crossfire* (1947), *Nightmare Alley* (1947), *Gentleman's Agreement* (1947), *Boy with The Green Hair* (1948), *Snake Pit* (1948), and *The Treasure of the Sierra Madre* (1948).

I didn't fully understand what Frank and Myrna were commiserating about. In 1947, the House Un-American Activities Committee (HUAC) had begun its assault on citizen rights of expression by attacking members of the movie industry, questioning their patriotism and whether they knew any Communists during the Great Depression.

Our blue-collar family in Berdoo had a TV back in those early days, thanks to our wealthy NYC relations. Many a late night I watched those Congressional Hearings with my mom, who repeatedly warned me about the dangers of speaking out in public. U.S. Senator Joe McCarthy's gruff demeanor was reason enough to keep one's trap shut. His beady-eyed legal beagle Roy Cohn was a scary reminder to remain invisible to the powers that be.

HUAC's efforts to demonize some people and certain ideas, as a means for preserving American freedom, actually had had a chilling effect on America's democracy and had stifled citizen participation nationwide to where almost half the public did not register to vote. One could argue that all the new governmental powers Congress granted President Harry Truman from 1946-47 were intended to keep the public out of governmental affairs. Formation in 1947 of the National Security Council (NSC) and its action arm Central Intelligence Agency (CIA) made invisible the machinations of international relations. The seeds of the Cold War were planted. Their strategy was to keep the public under control by promoting the fear of "spreading Communism" and by dangling above everyone's head the horrendous prospect of nuclear war. "Leave government to the savvy professionals" was their irrefutable message.

It took me years of watching the "Best movies ever made" — the movies Frank and Myrna talked about — to fully understand their lament — that being free helped you see the truth, and vice versa.

Those HUAC investigations of 1948 began America's official censoring of public film-making content — in complete disregard of our First Amendment Rights, and Frank and Myrna knew it. Judging by the opinion pages of the day, hardly anyone else did. For years, HUAC and its censoring institutions suppressed content, shaped public policy, created false cultural narratives, destroyed artistic standards, conducted unconstitutional behavior that ruined lives, and, maybe, even created wars. Everything HUAC did was designed to intimidate the public not to act, not to be free. To reduce your stress, you had the "freedom" to drink highly addictive alcohol, smoke cancer-causing cigarettes, and drop medically approved speed, all items taxable by the state. Only thing that helped you be free in those days was dancing to "colored" music. That's the way things were until The Sixties, when the Kennedy Brothers began to question authority.

At Campaign Headquarters the perennial group of young lawyers complained about the difficulty in obtaining passes to the Election Night Party to be held at The Factory, L.A.'s hippest nightclub. "It's where all the celebrities are going to be," they grumbled. "In Robert's Rules," whined a young L.A. County prosecutor pining for a business meeting of the Young Professionals, "they show how to write Articles of Incorporation."

As the California campaign was coming to a conclusion, I decided not to waste any time engaging these peripheral forces. Taking me away from campaign work was counterproductive. I understood that young lawyers didn't feel comfortable unless there was a contract to follow. Every night the young attorneys gathered at the Wilshire Blvd. Headquarters hoping for a speaking assignment. They looked like penguins out of water, wearing their three-piece suits, black shiny shoes, smoking Kent cigarettes, scanning left and right, making sure they didn't miss any celebrity sighting.

To be fair, there were activist-lawyers in the campaign. Bob Shapiro, a budding criminal lawyer, another of UCLA's notorious KELPS, wasn't shy about getting involved. In the closing days "Shaps" drove New York City Borough President Percy Sutton of Brooklyn to a string of South Central Coffee Klatches. Corporate banking lawyer Bob Thomson and his wife Kay hosted several Kennedy Coffee Klatches in Westwood. There were activists and there were poseurs. Robert Kennedy being a lightning rod, he attracted everyone.

After the June 1st TV Debate on KGO in San Francisco between Senators McCarthy and Kennedy, I was completely convinced of RFK's upcoming victory. McCarthy was too clean, too
vague, and way too cool a personality to lead all of America.
Even worse, reports came in that McCarthy had soiled himself and capitulated to Humphrey in an all-out effort to "STOP
Kennedy in California."

Thomas Finney, McCarthy's new campaign director, had been
with the CIA and was a law partner of Clark Clifford, LBJ's new
Secretary of Defense. Longtime McCarthy aide Andrew Robin-
son had sensed the coming betrayal; and on May 22nd started,
"Operation Change-Over to Kennedy!"

The Young Professionals' tables at Headquarters were humming with activity, scheduling Coffee Klatches as far away as
Fontana and Corona. The young lawyers called for a meeting at
Canter's Restaurant on nearby Fairfax Avenue to sort out "Future leadership issues and, hopefully, to elect Young Professionals' corporate officers."

Half a dozen young Jewish lawyers invite an Irish-Catholic activist to a famous Jewish Deli to discuss "corporate" business. Sensing a huge waste of time, after leaving Headquarters,
I drove west on Wilshire toward home. At Fairfax Boulevard,
instead of turning right to Canter's, I went left to Tom Bergin's
for an Irish coffee, or two . . . maybe it was three.

After California's June 4th Primary, there was only one more
Democratic Primary — June 18th, State of New York with its
large number of delegates.

The California campaign was obviously under control and
headed for victory. Personally, I saw myself in life as a scout,
working the outer edges of society, connecting different, but
like-minded, groups. Not a Mr. In-between, but a Mr. Go-be-
tween. And I didn't need no stinking party at The Factory to celebrate RFK's victory. The enjoyment was in the winning and in
that everyone was playing their part, making the New Frontier
an unstoppable worldwide force.

I decided my work in L.A. was done, and that I should go to New York to begin canvassing the scene there to see how California's grassroots campaign experience could best be replicated in NYC's concrete canyons.

Bill Philipp, a PCV from my Cornell CD group lived in Manhattan and invited me to stay with him and his wife as I scoped out the New York state primary. I figured my firsthand experience in how we whipped McCarthy in California would be positively received. I was *not* going back to educating businessmen for UCLA Extension. I was committing myself full-time to the campaign and to helping to right America's foundering ship of state. It was my duty as an American warrior. I had my shield, The Constitution, and my weapons, The Bill of Rights.

In order for me to be a part of the campaign to take back America, I had to be where the action was taking place. As a scout it was my job to be on the point of the spear.

I took ten days of vacation, and on June 2nd flew to NYC excited with the message I was carrying, and thrilled to be ahead of the first wave of activists who would be coming from California.

As I flew across country my mind drifted to November . . .

Election Day 1968 would be a formidable victory for The People: a black/white/brown, urban/rural, Christian/Jewish victory reflecting America's unique diversity! Key campaign players would sort through the spoils of victory, selecting jobs in which they could do the most good: Office of Economic Opportunity, Peace Corps, Agency for International Development, U.S. Park Service. Maybe my railroad experience would vault me into a challenging transportation opportunity . . .

I arrived in New York after dark. The City looked like an exquisite piece of Art Deco jewelry, sparkling in graphite with diamond lights. Manhattan's electrified silhouette, as seen from the Brooklyn Bridge, is my most cherished view of New York City, especially during a summer electrical storm.

The day of the California Primary I visited several Kennedy for President operations in Manhattan. There was some concern that the Oregon defeat might discourage some Kennedy voters from going to the polls.

In East L.A., Alberto Juárez was awakened early. Two-dozen NFW farm workers from Delano were at his front door ready to Get-Out-The-Vote *para Roberto*, "They knew exactly what they were doing," Alberto recalled, "guiding thousands to the polls. We planned to meet later in the evening at the Ambassador Hotel to *festiar* (party)."

That same night I took Bill and his wife Kathryn to dinner. I knew the Los Angeles County voter tabulations would take forever, so we decided to see the late showing of Stanley Kubrick's new film, *2001: A Space Odyssey*.

Before entering the movie theater, we heard at a newsstand that Kennedy had won rural South Dakota in a landslide. I was ecstatic. That was supposed to be Humphrey country. I felt as if I was riding the cusp of a rising wave of national reform.

The movie *2001* was a wild and absorbing intergalactic adventure far from politics. The movie was pure '68 . . . more complex than originally thought, and had a much longer lasting impact.

22

DEATH OF THE FUTURE

By the time we returned to the Philipp's Manhattan apartment and turned on the TV, Kennedy was standing at the podium in the Embassy Ballroom at the Ambassador Hotel, smiling bashfully. He had just claimed victory; everyone on stage was beaming. Kennedy read from his list of those he wanted to thank for making the victory possible, "Congressman Thomas Rees, Dolores Huerta . . .."

In fact, when the final tally was made, Robert Kennedy owed his California victory to the more than 200,000 Mexican Americans who had registered and voted, many who now saw themselves as Chicanos.

As I listened, I felt proud of being part of a massive grassroots effort by millions of nameless people dedicated to doing good. I was a simple, working-class guy who, through diligence, public education, and good timing, had found himself riding the crest of a national wave of reform. Not just any ordinary wave, but one of tsunami-magnitude, where America would restore its egalitarian course and reach out to the world, offering an intelligent and progressive answer for multi-cultural living here on Earth. This was America's destiny — to take our national reform movement worldwide.

After walking on the streets of Manhattan and riding the subways of Brooklyn, I knew Kennedy would win New York City easily. There was no way the political bosses at the Chicago Convention could override such popular support from all corners of the country. We, The People, would triumph in November. It was like we were riding with Robin Hood pursuing the noble goal of saving the Greenwood, which in this case meant, saving our Earthly environment from nuclear madness. To be part of such an historic peace movement was a working-class dream come true.

That fabulous euphoric feeling I felt in New York, of being right, of being righteous, lasted five minutes. The shot that killed him in the Ambassador Hotel's kitchen exploded my brain as well. I saw myself as an arrow of battle, and, of my own volition, I had sent myself flying across country to be in the thick of the upcoming June 18th New York primary, which now was totally meaningless. How had I gotten so far ahead of myself that I thought I knew the future?

Alberto Juárez was in the Ambassador's packed Embassy Ballroom reeling in happiness, when a man burst on to the stage yelling from the podium, "Is there a Doctor? Robert Kennedy has been shot."

Alberto said later it was unbelievable. Felt like a knife in the heart. "I had brought four beautifully attired teen-aged Kennedy Girls from East L.A. to enjoy the Victory party. They were hysterical, screaming and crying, but we couldn't leave. The police had closed off the exits. I had promised the girls' strict Catholic parents that I would have them home by midnight, but the girls and I were trapped in this horrible nightmare we couldn't escape."

UAW's Paul Schrade stopped the first bullet from Sirhan's gun with his forehead. He was one of five persons injured in the shooting. Olympian Rafer Johnson, after helping to wrestle the gun away from Sirhan, took the pistol home, emotionally wounded.

Jim Murray, sportswriter legend for the *Los Angeles Times*, cut to the chase, "Once again America the Beautiful has taken a bullet to the groin. . . .. The Violent States of America. One bullet is mightier than one million votes. It's not a Democracy; it's a lunacy."

For Dolores Huerta, it was tragedy, "I never thought I would see the death of the future."

The next day I wandered down Fifth Avenue weeping inconsolably. I had planned to buy Marie a piece of jewelry at Tiffany's to celebrate our 4th Wedding Anniversary. I stood there on Park Avenue, at the front door, but I could not enter. I could not purchase any gift for any reason.

My whole world of ending the war, of promoting peace throughout the world, had been blown to pieces by yet another lone assassin's bullet. Worse is that I had anticipated what life would bring, and only I knew of my travesty. I was so cocky I didn't even have to wait for the California Election results to leave for New York. Yes, RFK did win in California; and, yes, it was a smart idea to be ahead of the wave that would migrate to New York. I thought I would be out in front, actually making a contribution. Here I was in New York City, ready for action, but the primary campaign I had come to join was irrelevant.

I could barely speak to Bill and Kathryn as I left. I was so ashamed of counting my chickens before they had hatched. RFK died before my plane for LAX left.

I had had my Last Hurrah. I was through with election politics. Twice, my life had been upended by election results that were trumped by murder. My hopes for our country and for the world were dashed. I was angry, but there was no one to direct my anger at. As overly curious an individual as I am, I had zero interest in learning how RFK died. He was dead. The leader of our movement was gone. The nationwide effort was over. I was doubly sad. We would not have peace, and I proved that I could not stay in the present.

Marie suggested I stay in New York, and ride the funeral train to D.C., but I could not. The wild fever dream of ending the Vietnam War and of saving America was over. I had to move on.

But what was I going to do? Thanks to the Peace Corps I was a trained and experienced community organizer and, indeed, the Nation needed help at the grassroots. But there were no jobs for organizers. Community organizer was, amongst the landed gentry, a hated occupation. I felt lost. My whole life, which had great meaning, suddenly was empty.

Tens of thousands of New Yorkers lined the streets, circling St. Patrick's Cathedral on Fifth Avenue for 25 blocks for a chance to bid farewell to the martyred candidate. On June 8th, inside the Cathedral were more than 2,300 of the faithful, including 200 Catholic priests. Catholic respect doesn't get much higher than to have a battalion of priests praying for you.

They were not alone. A worldwide following mourned Robert Kennedy's murder.

His younger brother Senator Ted Kennedy's eulogy was simple and straightforward. He said Robert should be remembered "simply as a good and decent man, who saw wrong and tried to right it, saw suffering and tried to heal it, saw war and tried to stop it." The Senator's voice cracked in grief. He ended his eulogy with the same words his brother had used to signal to the press each time his speech would be over. Quoting George Bernard Shaw, the youngest Kennedy Brother repeated the call, "Some men see things as they are and say why? I dream things that never were and say, Why not?"

Huddled in front of the television, I painfully watched RFK's funeral train along with tens of millions of other mourners. As the day dragged on, I silently wept, drained of thought, grieved with psychic pain. Hundreds of thousands of Americans solemnly lined the 226 miles of railroad track from New York City to the Nation's Capital. His army of citizen-soldiers somberly stood and saluted him and his cohorts, as the 21-car funeral train slowly rumbled by.

Mankiewicz, conductor of RFK's last train ride, battled the fates — railway management, pedestrian deaths, and he even threatened to stop on the mainline unless they were given priority. Mank held strong; the train moved forward with green signals clearing the mainline to D.C's Union Station. Stoically, these railroad-track witnesses to his Presidential campaign paid their — and our Nation's — final respects to U.S. Senator Robert Francis Kennedy, candidate for President.

I did not regret my decision to go back to L.A.

The four-hour train trip to D.C. was four and a half hours late, arriving at Union Station long after the sun had set, meaning, the train's water-coolers were empty, snack bar closed, toilet tanks filled. There was no booze, unless you brought your own. I had to be realistic. What would I, an unknown campaign worker, say to the widow, "Remember the Ambassador's Party in Lima, back in '65, you and me and El Cordobés?" To be totally realistic, when it was all over, what would I have done in Arlington Cemetery at midnight? I could not intrude upon Frank's awful world.

I did miss hearing the many different musical groups, bands, and choirs who performed for Senator Kennedy's long funeral procession. In front of the Lincoln Memorial the U.S. Marine Corps Band gave a rousing rendition of "The Battle Hymn of the Republic," one of the Senator's favorite pieces. It was one of many versions sung that day in his honor, starting with his Eulogy at St. Patrick's cavernous Cathedral and Andy Williams' soulful a cappella version that filled it. From beginning to end, it was a Hero's Farewell.

A little after midnight the Kennedy Brothers were re-united in Arlington Cemetery, a stellar pair of Irish American Patriots of the 20th Century. They were the first, and only two veterans to be buried at Arlington in the dark.

23

MAKE A DIFFERENCE

I had never felt sadder in my life. Nor had I ever been so angry that I had to bury my real feelings. Intellectually, I could not explore who did this deed because the answer might push me off the cliff of respectability. I did not want to think members of our government, past or present, had been involved with his murder, or Martin's, or JFK's. I could not go there — thinking a group of citizens would subvert America's unique democracy for personal gain. A nation is far more important than any one of its groups. Our core document, the U.S. Constitution, claims we're all born with equal rights. Who would selfishly dishonor the noble cause of America's egalitarian experiment? I was an American warrior sworn to protect the Nation, but not to investigate it.

Instead, during the summer of 1968, as the world burst into revolution from Prague to Tokyo, I was an emotionless zombie, going through the motions at my office in UCLA's Graduate School of Business, planning the next round of imaginative short courses for business people.

At lunch, I sat alone in the adjacent Franklin D. Murphy Sculpture Garden, licking my wounds, hoping these frozen figures would inspire me to act.

Meanwhile, the violence to our nation and to the world continued shamelessly. The month of May had produced the most American fatalities of any month in the entire Vietnam War — 2,415 dead! That meant 80 American families a day were being destroyed. Keep in mind, out of all age groups, 18-year olds suffered the largest losses in the Vietnam War — 33,103. Is that not criminal to sacrifice the life of a young man just as it begins, a mere pawn in a high-stakes international game of dominos? What could one person do to stop the madness?

The Democratic Party's August 26–29th Presidential Nominating Convention in Chicago, televised live from gavel-to-gavel, turned into a bizarre Marquis de Sade nightmare.

Not to be outdone, the Chicago Police Department sunk as low as the LAPD and violently attacked unarmed peaceful protesters, citizens of mainly college age. Again, blood was spilt in public parks as armed public employees cowardly beat up the unarmed citizenry.

Inside the Convention Hall vitriol flowed freely. Chicago's Mayor Richard Daley frothed like a mad dog. If words could kill, no one would have survived the Chicago Democratic Convention.

Outside, Chicago PD's violent and willful brutality against those campaigning for peace reflected our military's over-kill mentality and its unrepentant never-ending bombing battle against defenseless Vietnamese peasants — their women, children, and elderly. America's experiment in democracy was going up in smoke, disgraced and dishonored, fighting all the wrong people for all the wrong reasons. How could the government get so far off track and act in such an un-American manner?

Despite all of the Convention's negativity — the physical violence, the vilification of the anti-Vietnam War delegates, the acceptance of Mississippi's segregated delegation — there was one redeeming element. At the end of the convention, they aired a thirty-two-minute documentary, "Remembering Robert Kennedy" by Charles Guggenheim. The Academy Award-winning short documentary contained a clip from a speech Senator Kennedy gave in South Africa on 6/6/1966 — the day South Africans were celebrating Re-Affirmation of Academic and Human Freedom.

As I watched him speak, a flutter inside my solar plexus suddenly alerted me. That speech had something to tell me. When I read the speech in full, I knew I had found the answer to my dilemma of what to do now that the peace movement's leadership had been murdered and America's future looked bleakest:

Few will have the greatness to bend history itself;
but each of us can work to change a small portion of

events, and in the total of all those acts will be written the history of this generation. Thousands of Peace Corps volunteers are making a difference in isolated villages and city slums in dozens of countries. Thousands of unknown men and women in Europe resisted the occupation of the Nazis and many died, but all added to the ultimate strength and freedom of their countries. It is from numberless diverse acts of courage and belief that human history is shaped. Each time a man stands up for an ideal, or acts to improve the lot of others, or strikes out against injustice, he sends forth a tiny ripple of hope, and crossing each other from a million different centers of energy and daring those ripples build a current which can sweep down the mightiest walls of oppression and resistance . . ..

On Earth, God's work must truly be our own.

RFK had closed his South African speech exactly as his brother John, The President, had closed his January 20, 1961 Inaugural Address. It was God's work we were doing.

I had no choice but to become "a tiny ripple of hope."

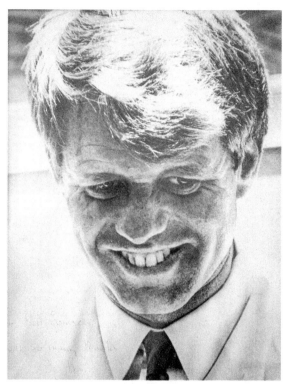

Senator Robert F. Kennedy

Photo by Jerry D. Alto, June 1, 1968. San Francisco CA

Inscribed "Christmas '68 Ethel Kennedy"

APPENDICES

APPENDICES

ADDENDUM

I. June 4, 1968 Democratic Primary: Peace was not a splinter group.

As far as democracy goes, California's Primary produced the highest voter turnout in state history. Out of 7,952,617 registered Democrats, 5,723,047 voted — 72.2%!

Robert Kennedy won with 1,472,166 votes, McCarthy was 2nd with 1,329,301, followed by the "no preference" delegation, 128,337 — headed by California's Lt. Governor Tom Lynch, a stand-in for Vice President Hubert Humphrey.

Even so, between RFK and McCarthy, 2,801,467 citizens voted for peace — half of all the Democrats who voted.

The statewide victory was decided in L.A. County where 71.34% of its registered voters turned out to vote, highest in county history! Of the 2,075,661 Primary election voters: 586,619 chose RFK's delegation, 463,928 chose McCarthy's. Between them, 1,050,547 citizens voted against the Vietnam War! Over 50% of the county's conservative voters wanted peace.

Statewide, RFK's margin of victory over McCarthy was 142,865. In L.A. County's 6,929 precincts, RFK beat McCarthy by 122,691 votes! Clearly, NFW getting out the vote and John Lewis and his cohorts working South Central by day and the Westside by night were as instrumental as the Kennedy Coffee Klatches in sealing RFK's winner-take-all victory.

Most remarkably, Senator Kennedy, running against two opponents (McCarthy and Lynch), won with 586,619 votes, beating the top GOP name on the L.A. County ballot, a local who, running unopposed, garnered only 512,126 votes. As a side-note, RFK kicked Governor Ronald Reagan's ass in L.A.

County as well. Election-wise, California's Democratic Primary election was a precedent-setting grass roots victory.

II. The Decline in Partisanship & the Rise of the Invisible Voter Reform Movement

CALIFORNIA VOTER REGISTRATION BY PARTY: 1968–2020

YEAR	DEM.	REP.	NO PARTY*	3RDPARTY**
1968 June	54.9%	40.3%	2.2%	2.5%
1972	56.0	36.0	4.8	1.2
1976	57.3	34.7	5.6	2.4
1980	53.2	34.7	9.4	2.7
1984	52.0	36.5	9.1	2.4
1988	50.4	38.6	8.9	2.1
1992	49.1	37.0	10.3	3.5
1996	46.9	36.8	11.2	5.1
2000	45.4	34.9	14.2	5.3
2004	43.5	34.7	17.7	4.6
2008	44.4	31.1	19.5	4.3
2012	43.7	29.4	20.9	6.0
2016	44.9	26.0	24.3	4.8
2018 June	44.4	25.1	25.5 ***	5.6
2020	46.1	24.2	24.0	5.7

Statistical Source: CA Secretary of State archives.

    * Replaced "Decline to State Political Preference."
    ** American Independent Party, Peace & Freedom Party, and Green Party.
    *** First time non-partisan voters constituted 2nd largest group of registered voters.

A BRIEF BIO

While working as a railroad switchman, the author earned a BA in political theory at UCLA. Inspired by JFK he joined the Peace Corps who trained him to be a social change agent in the Andes of Peru.

Upon his return, he joined UCLA's Urban Crisis program and helped create community development projects in Pico-Union (low-income housing) and Venice Beach (heroin treatment), while earning a Masters in Community Development: "University as a Resource to Low-Income Community Problem Solvers."

When Governor Reagan de-funded University of California's Urban Crisis program, the author continued as an independent activist and program evaluator for another 30 years, helping non-profit organizations: Pico-Union Neighborhood Council, Tuum Est, Venice Drug Coalition, Venice Town Council, Voter Registration Program, Born Again KELPS, Venice Cityhood Survey.

To publicize these non-partisan projects, he became a freelance commentator adopting the nom de plume of Sweet William. *Los Angeles Times* editors have described him as a "poet," "philosopher," "romantic," even a "closet thrill-seeker."

Sweet William is currently working on his memoir, *Autobiography of an Activist: A Serendipitous Journey from Brooklyn to Venice Beach.*

WHAT'S NEXT

JFK & RFK MADE ME DO IT: 1960-1968 is the prologue to
*AUTOBIOGRAPHY OF AN ACTIVIST: A Serendipitous Journey
from Brooklyn to Venice Beach,* a work in progress by activ-
ist-writer Sweet William of Venice, CA.

Autobiography Of An Activist is an in-depth look into the
world of social activism and what it takes to be a change agent.
It provides theoretical and tactical information to use in building a community of action, as well as an understanding of the
spiritual role of the public benefit activist.

Emerging from this examination of a lifetime of community actions is a wealth of problem-solving strategies. Often they
are commonsense approaches, simple tactics and techniques the
author has gleaned from his lifetime of working with more than
30 public benefit activists of every imaginable socio-econom-
ic-cultural composition.

All of these change agents worked to solve community problems of national import, from heroin addiction to police abuse,
from the lack of low-income housing to creating park space with
urban renewal, from providing juvenile delinquent prevention
programs to empowering voters by decentralizing large urban
cities and breaking them into smaller civic entities. All of the
independent activists that populate this Brooklyn-to-Venice-
Beach narrative hold in common their pursuit of a sustainable
world of peace where one has the freedom and the opportunity
to be Bob Marley-happy.

While community actions are the spine of this grass roots
story, a surprising discovery about the voting populace was
made. Rejection of political parties by registered voters has become a national trend that the media has refused to acknowl-

edge. This non-partisan shift proves U.S. voters have not given up on the American experiment. (See Addendum, part II, page 218 — "The Decline in Partisanship & the Rise of the Invisible Voter Reform Movement: 1968-2020").

The *Autobiography's* concluding chapter sets forth a "Constitutional Caper," a simple and legal solution for solving America's woes: economical, environmental, and ethical. By employing this constitutionally sanctioned plan, our Nation will be able to restore its leadership role in the world community as an egalitarian force in strong support of equal opportunities for all.

ACKNOWLEDGMENTS

Regardless of how much pre-planning one attempts, writing a book is an invitation into the unknown, entering unexplored pathways that often reveal secrets, both yours and your culture's. It is a big undertaking, especially dealing with those unexpected storylines and facts.

At the end of this unpredictable process, I have a far richer outcome than originally anticipated. Hence there's a great deal of appreciation to be passed out to those who helped this book and its secrets come to life.

Much appreciation goes to Gonzalo Emilio Romero Sommer, whose doctoral dissertation (State University of New York — Stony Brook) focused on the Mantaro Valley Rural Electric Cooperative, a project I had worked on during my Peace Corps service in Peru from 1964 to 1966.

When Gonzalo reached out to me in December of 2018, it was the first I had heard that the Electric Cooperative that I had worked on had been funded, just two weeks after I left Peru on June 6, 1966. Thanks to Gonzalo, I learned the Mantaro Valley Rural Electric Cooperative catalyzed the development of Peru's Andean electrical resources, the first building block of Peru's entire rural electrical system. I'm extraordinarily grateful to Gonzalo for letting me know that my work as a Peace Corps Volunteer had a positive and lasting effect.

I decided then and there to write this book about what happened fifty-two years ago, as a reminder to today's activists of where we've been. I would use the Kennedy Brothers own words to tell the story of their push for peace in the Sixties, and how that affected my life choices.

If Gonzalo planted the seed for this book, Marian Haley Beil, publisher of Peace Corps Writers, is its mother, as she magically transformed my original pamphlet idea into a smart 23-chapter book. She worked tirelessly to fact check, organize, and edit, adding photos and maps. Besides me, no one else has invested as much time, talent, and intellect into this endeavor. My appreciation will be never ending.

Ron Arias, a former writer at *People Magazine* and a Peace Corps Volunteer in Peru from 1963 to 1965 whom I interviewed for this book, also provided me with a key insight into Peruvian life, something I had failed to address when I first started writing. After our interview, he sent me a copy of his 2003 memoir *Moving Target: A Memoir of Pursuit* (Bilingual Press). While waiting for Marian's final edit, I decided to read his chapter on Cusco, Peru, capital of the ancient Inca Empire. I was soon shocked to discover he witnessed a massacre of Quechua-speaking Native Americans. This little-known incident was emblematic of centuries of harsh treatment endured by the Andean people at the hands of colonial and post-colonial forces. It was these very conditions that JFK and his Alliance for Progress attempted to address. So I'm more than happy to acknowledge that Ron helped me fill a hole in my storyline that I didn't even know existed. He didn't tell me to read about Cusco; he just knew that if I read his Cusco story I would soon discover the nasty secret of why Peru's Incan descendants are murdered and no one cares.

I'm deeply grateful to Dolores Huerta, UFW co-founder, and recipient of the Presidential Medal of Freedom, and many other social justice awards, who generously took time for an interview. She saluted the role the Community Service Organization (CSO) played in establishing the Chicano Movement. She also described how her style of home-based organizing and the farm labor movement's intersect with RFK. Sharing her many experiences added a rich authenticity to my Brown Power narrative.

I've read my share of books about JFK and RFK, and I'm indebted to those authors who provided me with on-site details to events I did not attend, but who nevertheless assisted me in the re-telling of Robert Kennedy's inspiring 1968 run for the Presidency (see *Bibliography*, page 239).

Numerous Peace Corps Volunteers and staff were generous with their time, as were those outside the Peace Corps community whom I interviewed (see *Interviewees*, pages 229–231).

I wish to extend my thanks to JFK Library Archivist Abigail Malangone, who, at the height of the COVID-19 pandemic, slipped into the archives to ascertain the dates of RFK's travel schedule while touring Peru and Chile in November 1965. Thanks to Michael Desmond for his help in gathering together JFK speeches.

Much appreciation also to Caroline Angel Burke, Vice President of the Edward M. Kennedy Institute for the United States Senate, who went to Hyannis Port in late 2020 to look on the back of the Kennedy family's favorite photo of Robert Kennedy to find out for me who the photographer was. She reported that it was USN Lt. Jerry D. Alto, and the photo was taken in San Francisco on June 1, 1968, facts I had been trying to find for decades. A special thanks to Lt. Alto for taking this iconic image, a stunning photo that would appear in newspaper stories remembering RFK, the photo that his widow Ethel sent to those in the 1968 campaign, hand-signed with the message "Christmas '68 Ethel Kennedy." His iconic photo is published here for the first time with his photographer credit.

Finally, as an immigrant from Brooklyn, a blue-collar worker from Berdoo, and a closet dyslexic, I was fortunate that my wife Barbara, being a veteran English teacher, kept me in the right tense and employing the fewest number of words. Even late at night, confronted with a grammatical fork in the road, "Major Barbara" had just the right advice. Writing a book is no different than anything else: happy wife means happy life. Happiness is writing a story of discovery in a loving environment. May such bounties visit your life as well.

Sweet William
Lower Hollywood
July 26, 2021

INTERVIEWEES (IN PERSON)

James Bennett	Max Factor website
Lucy Berner Salenger	Mankiewicz Assistant
Irv Bernstein, Ph.D.	UCLA Political Science
William Brazill	Mendocino
Bernard Brodie, Ph.D.	UCLA/RAND Corp.
Marv Brody	UAW
Gerald Chaleff	Los Angeles Police Commission
Captain Kent Ewing	USS AMERICA CV 66
Davis Factor	Chairman, Max Factor
Russell Fitzgibbon, Ph.D.	UCLA Political Science
Phil Friedman	ASUCLA/IBM
James K. Galbraith, Ph.D.	The University of Texas at Austin
Norman Gall	*Commentary Magazine*
Richard J. Glasscock, M.D.	UCLA Medical School
Jules Glazer	RFK California Campaign Accountant
U.S. Senator Barry Goldwater (R)	Royce Hall, UCLA
Richard Goodwin	Alliance for Progress, Architect
Jay Gotfredson	Century City Anti-War Protestor
Felix Gutiérrez, Ph.D.	*La Raza* archives
Dolores Huerta	UFW Co-Founder
Walter Jenkin, Ph.D.	UCLA Political Science

Rafer Johnson	UCLA/Young Professionals for Kennedy
John Wesley Jones	U. S. Ambassador to Peru
Alberto Juárez	UMAS "Chair"
Nick Juárez	Ralph Guzmán confidant
John Lewis	Former Chairman, SNCC
William Marshall	co-star, *Catch My Soul*
George Murphy	VP, Technicolor & actor
Willard Murray	Aide, State Sen. Mervyn Dymally
William Norris	RFK's California Campaign Manager
Victor Palmieri	Deputy Director, Kerner Commission
Nelson Rising	O'Melveny & Myers
Gonzalo Romero Sommer Ph.D.	Peruvian Historian
Walt Whiteman Rostow, Ph.D.	LBJ's National Security Advisor
Stephen Saltzman	Temple Isaiah, Los Angeles
Irving Sarnoff	Organizer, Century City Anti-Vietnam War March
Bob Shapiro	UCLA
Richard Sherwood	Committee for California
Joel Siegel	UCLA
Roger D. Stone	*Time Magazine*
Robert Thomson	Young Professionals for Kennedy
Alejandro Toledo, Ph.D.	President of Peru, 2001–06
Martin Turnball	Schwab's Pharmacy
William vanden Heuvel	RFK Aide
Lee van Leeuwen	UCLA/Dictaphone
Carmen Warschaw	CA Democratic Party Leader
Jules Witcover	Journalist/Author

INTERVIEWEES (PEACE CORPS)

Volunteers:

Ron Arias

David J. Boyd

Catherine DeLorey

Jerry Drake

Jack Epstein

Marie Evensen

Michael Heyn

Marilyn Keyes

Evelyn Kohl de la Torre

Ralph Laird

Marjorie Lam Leon

Karen Marcus

Nancy Deeds Meister

Joel Meister

William Philipp

Stephen Russo

Alan Stanchfield

Harriet "Skeeter" Tower

Ken Wilmarth

Michael Wolfson

Staff:

Eugene Baird

Sam Guarnaccia

James "Jim" Lowry

Frank "Mank" Mankiewicz

Bill Moyers, Deputy Director

Thorburn "Trip" Reid

SPANISH-ENGLISH GLOSSARY

aficionados   fan, follower

Alianza para de Progresso   Alliance for Progress — President Kennedy's aid program for South America

altiplano   plateau above the tree-line

anchovy al fresco   fresh anchovy

apu   Inca sacred mountain

banderillas   little flags — thin, 30" long, 1" wide poles wrapped in colored paper anchored with a 1" steel barb used by the matador

barriada(s)   shanty town

barricada   barricade

balcon   balcony

bodega bag   animal-skin wine bag

borracho   drunk

caciques   princes of the Inca Empire

campesinos   peasant farmer

Campo Alegre   Camp Happy

capitan   captain

caudillo   mestizo military culture

Cerro Rico   rich mountain

cerviche   marinated fresh fish or shrimp eaten raw

chakra   field

compadres   friends

comunal   community owned

cooperación   working together

Cooperativísmo   an economic model based in part on
the Incan practice of community work (faena) and shared
ownership of the resulting end product

Cooperación Popular   President Belaúnde's new community
action agency patterned after the U.S. Peace Corps

copitas de aguardiente   shot glasses of firewater/schnapps

coraje   courage

corridas del toros   bullfight

cuyes   guinea pigs

curandaras   healers

desgraciadamente   unfortunately

despedida   farewell

el consejo del junta comunal   advice of the Community
Council

el Cordobés   a person from Córdoba, Spain

el dictador del Peru   Don Enrique Meiggs, who emerged as a
successful railroad builder

el hermano de JFK   brother of JFK

El hermano de JFK me dío este regalo personalmente   a
personal gift from the brother of JFK

*El Parque de Leyendas (*Park of Legends)   Lima's Zoological
Park

estera   straw mats

faena   citizens donating work to a community project

Fabrica de Cemento   cement factory

favela (Portugese)   shanty town

feria   festival

Ferrocarril Central   Central Railroad with 266-mile track
from Lima to Huancayo. Station stops are: Callao-Lima-
Huancayo-Huancavelica once a month

Ferrocarillo Sur   southern rail line from Cusco to Puno to
Arequipa

festiar   to party

fiscal   treasurer

futbol   soccer

gente decente   nice, upper-class people

gringos   North Americans, Europeans

guacos   ancient pre-Colombian pottery

guano   bird excrement (derived from the Quechua word
huanu)

Guardia Civil   local police

guayras (Quechua)   ovens

guerrilleros   revolutionary fighters

hacienda   large ranch

hijos   children

hijas de JFK   daughters of JFK, women PCVs

hijos de JFK   children of JFK – Peace Corps Volunteers

huanu (Quechua)   bird excrement

huaynos (Quechua)   Indigenous folk dances

Huayna Capac   11th Inca (emperor)

Iglesia Santiago Apostol   Catholic Church of Apostle James

Inca   see *Sapa Inca*

Instituto de Peruano-Norteamericano   US-Peru cooperating educational institute in Lima

Isla Blanca   White Island – volcanic island located at the mouth of Chimbote Bay, near Chimbote, Peru.

khipus (Quechua)   Inca Empire bookkeeping system of knotted colored strings

junta comunal   village community council

La Cooperativa   Mantaro Valley Rural Electric Cooperative (Huancayo)

La Corona Española   Spanish Crown

las comunidadas olvidadas   forgotten communities

la comunidad   the community

la entrevista para los siete   interview for seven

la montaña   Amazon Jungle side of the Andes

las tres gringas   three North American women

Lago de Titicaca   Lake Titicaca

latinoamericanos   Latin Americans

lomo saltado   seasoned steak strips with bell peppers, onions *lujo*   luxury

lustrador de zapatos   shoeshine boy

macho   manly

margen derecha   right side of a river

margen izquierda   left side of a river

madrina   godmother

mais que nada (Portuguese)   better than nothing

matador   bullfighter

mato grosso (Portuguese)   deep jungle

mestizos   people of mixed ancestry of Spanish adventurers and Indigenous women

mit'a (Quechua)   donation of work to a communal project and sharing in its outcome

mita (Spanish)   forced conscripted labor

ombligo   navel

once   (pronounced OWN-say)   #11; or drinking shot glasses of firewater (*aguardiente*) at 4pm, and so named *once* for aguardiente's 11 letters.

padrino   godfather

paiche   largest scaled freshwater fish in the world

pampa   flat lands

Parque de las leyendas   Park of Legends

papa a la huancaina   boiled potatoes in sauce de Huancayo

personalmente   personally

posta sanitaria   a small health station

puerto   port

¿Que pasa aqui?   What's going on here?

Quechua   the language of Caral ethnic group, an early settlement pre-Peru, 5,000 B.C.E.; language of the Inca civilization, 1250–1534; official modern language of Bolivia, Ecuador, and Peru.

San Cristóbal   St. Christopher

Sapa Inca (Quechua)   sole ruler of the Inca empire

Señor de los Milagros Feria   Lord of Miracles [Christ] Festival, takes place during October and two weeks of November.

Serrano   Andean inhabitant

Sicaínos — those living in Sicaya

sierra   mountains

socio   member

socios   members

soles   monetary denomination, approximately S/8 = US $1

sopa criolla   spicy soup

Sumaq urqu (Quechua)   *Beautiful Mountain*

tambo (Quechua)   rest stop

Teatro Colón   one of the world's 10 best opera houses located in Buenos Aires

tienda   small store often with a dirt floor

toreador   bull fighter

tragos y chicha   shots of aguardiente and glasses of Inca-style corn beer *un indio*   Indigenous person

viajeros   travelers

Virreinato del Peru   Viceroyalty of Peru

Virreinatos   Vice Royalties

un gringo de Cuerpo de Paz   Peace Corps Volunteer

ACRONYMS

ACLU American Civil Liberties Union

AFL-CIO American Federation of Labor and Congress of Industrial Organizations

ASUCLA Associated Students of UCLA

AWOC Agriculture Workers Organizing Committee 1966-72

CE common (or current) era

CIA U.S. Central Intelligence Agency

CRC Community Relations Committee, preceded the Jewish Federation of Greater Los Angeles

CSO Community Service Organization, a Mexican American civil rights organization

GNP Gross National Product

HUAC House Un-American Activities Committee

IAI Industrial Areas Foundation

JFK U.S. President John Fitzgerald Kennedy

KELPS Knights, Earls, Lords, Potentates, Sultans

LAPD Los Angeles Police Department

LAX Los Angeles International Airport

LBJ U.S. President Lyndon Baines Johnson

MAPA Mexican American Political Association

MASP   Mexican American Study Project

NCAA   National Collegiate Athletic Association

NFW   National Farm Workers (In 1972 the NFW became United Farm Workers of America. The UFWA is often printed without the A.)

NFWOC   National Farm Workers Organizing Committee (1966–72)

OEO   Office of Economic Opportunity (federal agency)

PCV   Peace Corps Volunteer

RFK   U.S. Senator Robert Francis Kennedy

RPCV   Returned Peace Corps Volunteer

SANE   National Committee for Sane Nuclear Energy

SDS   Students for a Democratic Society

SER   Service-Employment-Redevelopment

UAW   United Auto Workers

UCLA   University of California, Los Angeles

UCSC   University of California, Santa Cruz

UCSD   University of California, San Diego

UFW   United Farm Workers, authorized union of the AFL-CIO. Formed in 1972 with the merger of AWOC and NFWOC by the four co-founders: Andy Imutan, Larry Itilong, Dolores Huerta and César Chávez.

UMAS   United Mexican American Students

USC   University of Southern California

JOHN F. KENNEDY SPEECHES 1960–1963

Acceptance for Democratic Nominating for President, July 15, 1960. Los Angeles Memorial Coliseum. (video and print)
https://www.jfklibrary.org/learn/about-jfk/historic-speeches/acceptance-of-democratic-nomination-for-president

Inaugural Address, January 20, 1961. U.S. Capitol. D.C. (video and print)
https://www.jfklibrary.org/learn/about-jfk/historic-speeches/inaugural-address

Address on the First Anniversary of the Alliance for Progress, March 13, 1962. White House. D.C. (print)
https://www.presidency.ucsb.edu/documents/address-the-first-anniversary-the-alliance-for-progress

American University Commencement Address. "A Strategy of Peace." June 10, 1963. D.C. (video excerpt and print)
https://www.jfklibrary.org/learn/about-jfk/historic-speeches/american-university-commencement-address

Televised Address to the Nation on Civil Rights, June 11, 1963. Oval Office, White House. D.C. (video excerpt and print)
https://www.jfklibrary.org/learn/about-jfk/historic-speeches/televised-address-to-the-nation-on-civil-rights

BIBLIOGRAPHY

BOOKS

Arias, Ron. *Moving Target – A Memoir of Pursuit.* Tempe, AZ: Bilingual Press, Arizona State University, 2003.

Arias, Ron. *My Life as a Pencil.* St. Paul, MN: Red Bird Chap Books, 2015.

Baker, Russ. *Family of Secrets.* New York, NY: Bloomsbury Press, 2008.

Bernstein, Irving. *The Lean Years — A History of the American Worker: 1920-1933,* Boston: Houghton Mifflin, 1960, with Frances Fox Piven.

Bruck, Connie. *When Hollywood Had A King.* New York, NY: Random House, 2003.

Cohen, Andrew. *Two Days in June – John F. Kennedy and the 48 Hours That Made History.* Toronto, Ontario, Canada: McClelland & Stewart, 2014.

Crenshaw, M.D., Charles A. *JFK: Conspiracy of Silence.* New York, NY: Penguin Books, 1992.

David, Lester *Ethel, The Story of Mrs. Robert F. Kennedy.* New York, NY and Cleveland, OH: The World Publishing Company, 1971.

Douglass, James W. *JFK and the Unspeakable.* Maryknoll, NY: Orbis Books, 2008.

English, T. J. *Havana Nocturne.* New York, NY: Harper Collins Publishing, 2007.

Escobar Moscoso, Gabriel. *Sicaya: Cambios Culturales en una Comunidad Mestiza Andina*. Doctoral Dissertation, Cornell University, NY, 1968.

Flores-Ochoa, Jorge and Valencia, Abraham E. *Rebeliones indigenas, quechuas y aymaras: homenaje al bicentenario de la rebelion campesina de Tupac Amaru, 1780–1980*. Cuzco, Peru: Centro de Estudios Andinos Cuzco, 1980.

Fulsom, Don. *Nixon's Darkest Secrets: The Inside Story of America's Most Troubled President*. New York, NY: Thomas Dunne Books, 2012; *The Mafia's President: Nixon and the Mob*. New York, NY: Thomas Dunne Books, St. Martin's Press, 2012.

Goodwin, Richard N. *Remembering America*. Boston, Toronto: Little, Brown and Company, 1988.

Gonzales, Gilbert G. "My First Lessons in Chicano History Were Heard at the Kitchen Table," interview by Gilda L. Ochoa. *Radical History Review*, Fall 2008.

Groden, Robert J. *The Killing of a President*. New York, NY: Viking Penguin Books, 1993.

Guthman, Edwin O. and Shulman, Jeffrey. (Editors) *Robert Kennedy In His Own Words*. New York, NY: Bantam Press, 1988.

Halberstam, David. *The Unfinished Odyssey of Robert Kennedy*. New York, NY: Random House, 1968.

Hevner, Peter. *William R. Grace: The Pirate of Peru*. New York, NY: 1888.

Kaiser, Charles. *1968 In America*. New York, NY: Weidenfeld & Nicolson, 1988.

Kennedy, Robert F. *To Seek A Newer World*. Garden City, NY: Doubleday & Company, Inc., 1967.

Lane, Mark. *Rush to Judgment*. New York, NY: Holt, Rinehart & Winston, 1966.

Lowry, James H. *Change Agent: A Life Dedicated to Creating Wealth for Minorities.* Bloomington, IN: Archway Publishing, 2020.

Mankiewicz, Frank. *So As I was Saying. . ..* New York, NY: Thomas Dunne Books, St. Martin's Press, 2016.

Palermo, Joseph. *In His Own Right – The Political Odyssey of Senator Robert Kennedy.* New York, NY: Columbia University Press, 2001.

Rabe, Stephen G. *The Most Dangerous Area in the World: John F. Kennedy Confronts Communist Revolution in Latin America.* Chapel Hill, NC: University of North Carolina Press, 1999.

Romero Sommer, Gonzalo. *Alternating Currents: Political and Hydroelectri Power in Peru, 1895-1975.* Doctoral Dissertation. Stony Brook University, NY, 2021.

Ross, Sr., Fred. *Axioms for Organizers by Fred Ross, Sr., Trailblazer for Social Justice.* Ebook, 2018

Schlesinger, Arthur Jr. *RFK and His Times.* New York, NY: Houghton-Mifflin, 1978.

Sheehan, Neil, Ellsberg, Daniel, and others. *The Pentagon Papers. New York*, NY: Bantam, 1971.

Sheffield, Glenn. *Peru and the Peace Corps, 1962-1968.* Doctoral Dissertation, University of Connecticut, 1991.

Stewart, Watt. *Henry Meiggs: Yankee Pizarro.* Durham, NC: Duke Press, 1946

Talbot, David. *Brothers: The Hidden History of the Kennedy Years.* New York, NY: Free Press, 2007.

Textor, Robert. *Cultural Frontiers of the Peace Corps: 5-Year Plan.* Boston, MA: MIT Press, 1966.

Thomas, Evan. *Robert Kennedy – His Life.* New York, NY: Simon & Schuster, 2000.

Tye, Larry. *Bobby Kennedy – The Making of a Liberal Icon.* New York, NY: Random House, 2016.

Valentine, Douglas. *The Strength of the Wolf: The Secret History of America's War on Drugs.* New York, NY/London, England: Verso, 2006.

vanden Heuvel, William and Gwirtzman, Milton. *On His Own: RFK 1964-68.* Garden City, NY: Doubleday & Company, Inc., 1970.

Witcover, Jules. *85 Days: The Last Campaign of Robert F. Kennedy.* New York, NY: Putnam Publications Group, 1969. *The American Vice Presidency: From Irrelevance to Power.* Washington, DC: Smithsonian Institution Press, 2014.

Zoellner, Tom. *Train: Riding the Rails That Created the Modern World.* New York, NY: Penguin Books, 2014.

COLLECTIONS, ARTICLES & VIDEO
Beede, Michael J. "Death at Tinta." *PeaceCorpsWorldwide. org.* March 24, 2021.

Bernstein, Shana. "A Cultural History of Jews in California – The Jewish Role in American Life, An Annual Review." Civic Defense to Civil Rights, The Growth of Jewish American Interracial Civil Rights Activism in Los Angeles, USC, Vol. 7, 2009.

Cal State Northridge: Urban Archives Center, Oviatt Library, CSO, 1949-50 Folder, Sec. AII Series III.

Deruy, Emily. "Community Organizer Fred Ross, Sr. Through the Years." *ABC News,* March 18, 2013.

Drew, Robert, director. *Crisis: Behind A Presidential Commitment.* Film documentary. ABC News, Drew Associates, 1963. Video.

Food & Agriculture Organization of the United Nations. *Peasant Participation in Community Reforestation, Four Communities in the Department of Cuzco, Peru*; Case Study Series #7. 1993.

Gall, Norman. "Letter From Peru." *Commentary Magazine,* June 1964.

Gonzales, Shmuel. "Resolving Conflict and Preventing Racial Violence, in the Classic Eastside." *BarrioBoychik.com*, July 2, 2016.

Guzmán, Ralph. "The Gentle Revolutionaires, Brown Power." *L.A. Times West Magazine*, January 26, 1969, page 9.

Guzmán, Ralph. CRC Minutes, "Tax Exempt." Cal State Northridge, Urban Archives Center, Oviatt Library 1949-50 folder, p. 63, February 25, 1950 and August 31, 1950.

Kirkendall, Andrew J. "Kennedy Men and the Fate of the Alliance for Progress in the LBJ Era, Brazil and Chile." *Diplomacy and Statecraft Journal*, 2007.

Mankiewicz, Frank. "Peace Corps — A Revolutionary Force." U.S. Peace Corps, Washington, D.C. 1962.

Metcalfe, Bill. "The Sapa Inca." *HistorysHistories.com.*

Meyerson, Harold. "The Legacy of Paul Schrade – Not Just the Other Guy Who Was Shot in the Ambassador Kitchen." *The American Prospect*, June 7, 2018.

Montgomery, T. Eglinton. "A Railroad in the Clouds." *Scribner's*, Vol. XIV #29, August, 1877.

PBS. "La Raza, Taking Back the Schools." PBS Documentary Series Video: "The Chicano Civil Rights Movement," 1996.

Pleasure, Thomas. "The Peace Corps Radicalized Me." A review of Frank Mankiewcz's posthumously published memoir, *So As I Was Saying, The Argonaut*, June 1, 2016; PeaceCorps Worldwide.org, June 3, 2016.

Schrade, Paul. Oral History: "The Civil Rights History Project." Interview about his career with the UAW and his involvement with the United Farm Workers, Robert Kennedy's presidential campaign and the antiwar and civil rights movement, 1989-90." 2 cassette tapes. Wayne State University. Walter P. Reuther Library

Stanford University, Palo Alto, CA, Special Collections: CSO Memo April 18, 1951, Folder 6, Box 5, Fred Ross Collection (CSO 1949-1957).

Stanford University, Palo Alto, CA, Special Collections: CSO Program, 1949, folder 11, Box 5, Fred Ross Collection (CSO 1949-1957).

UFW Collections. Walter Reuther Library of Labor and Urban Affairs, Wayne State University, Indiana.

UNPUBLISHED STORIES BY SWEET WILLIAM
"Chug-a-luggin and Other Acts of Andean Beer Drinking Etiquette." © 2019.

"Peace Corps Vacation: Eight-Day Amazon Jungle Walking Tour." © 2008.

"Peace Corps Journal." June 18, 1964–July 15, 1966.

HEAVY MEDIA

"Peru: Escalation in the Highlands"
Roger D. Stone, *Time Magazine*, 8/27/1965

After three months of fighting in the remote Andean highlands of central Peru, the Communist bands that President Fernando Belaúnde-Terry once dismissed as a "mere fiction" still operate. They are now a recognized fact of life. The constitutional guarantees suspended two months ago, putting the country under a form of martial law, are still suspended. Last week the Peruvian Congress went a step farther by authorizing military courts to impose the death penalty on captured guerrillas, and voted $7,400,000 to step up an already major operation against what the lawmakers called "imperialistic Communist aggression."

A Military Swarm. At first, the Peruvian government thought that rural police units could handle the Communists. It turned out to be too big a job, and now the army has taken over. The departmental capital of Huancayo, 120 miles east of Lima near the heart of guerrilla activity, swarms with soldiers and military vehicles. On nearby air fields, military transports land with supplies, while helicopters and bomb-laden twin-jet Canberra bombers stand ready for takeoff. In the field some 1,500 soldiers–advised by U.S. anti-guerrilla experts–are committed against the Red terrorists.

In a coordinated attack earlier this month, Canberra bombers swept in to blast a guerrilla stronghold near Pucará, a tiny village 90 miles from Huancayo. Ground forces overran the encampment, killing 20 guerrillas, but another 40 managed to escape. A few days later, another will-o-the-wisp band of guerrillas attacked the village of Satipo, only 70 miles away, killing two policemen and a civilian before fading back into the hills.

Indian Fatteners. The best estimate is that the guerrillas are in four bands, totaling possibly 1,000 men, and strongest in the area around Huancayo. Their leaders are Communist professionals: Guillermo Lobaton, 34, a Peruvian trained in insurgency in Cuba and Red China and reported to have fought with the Viet Cong, and Castroite Lawyer Luis de la Puente, 36, wanted in Lima for a 1962 murder. The terrorists preach the usual Communist line about capitalist exploitation and free land for all, attempt to counter the government's own considerable efforts at aid and social reform among the Indians by warning that free flour is distributed merely to fatten the Indians, the better to make soap of them later.

While the agitators have so far largely eluded the government's troops, they have at the same time failed to provoke a popular uprising among the masses. Few of the Indians have fallen for the line. Those who have joined up have responded to a more down-to-earth approach: payment of 1,000 soles, or $37, which in the highlands of Peru is more money than an Indian ordinarily expects to see in a year.

"Peace Corpsmen in Peru Attack U.S. Aid Policy"
By Dan Kurzman, *Washington Post* Staff Writer, 11/14/1965

Lima, Nov. 13 — In a tiny Indian Village in the Peruvian Andes, Sen. Robert F. Kennedy (D-N.Y.) climbed a ladder to the second floor of a partially constructed schoolhouse and through a glassless window congratulated the people for their effort to educate their children.

A Peace Corps official in the audience remarked: "The trouble is we're not helping them to do it."

Peace Corps representatives had deliberately brought Kennedy, who is touring South America, to see the half-built schoolhouse — on which no work had been done for a year — in order to impress him with what they consider the "folly" of current U.S. aid policy in Peru.

This effort symbolized the sharp split among U.S. officials in Peru on the question of aid pointed up a significant reason for the present wave of anti-Americanism here.

ECONOMIC PRESSURE SEEN
On the one hand, some officials make no secret of the fact that aid has been reduced as a means of pressuring the Peruvian Government into agreeing to an investment contract with the International Petroleum Co., owned by Standard Oil of New Jersey, that the Peruvians are reluctant to accept. Such pressure, they say, is justified as a measure to promote the success of their Alliance for Progress.

On the other hand, Peace Corps leaders and some representative of the Agency for International Development (AID) strongly maintained that the U.S. Government has no business exerting economic pressure on the Peruvian Government to accept a solution that it does not want.

"It's a damn shame that we have reduced our help to Peruvians, who are so willing to help themselves, especially since this is a democratic government," said Trip Reid, a Peace Corps official here. "I thought this was what the Alliance for Progress was all about."

AID CUT NOT PUBLICIZED

This point of view was constantly hammered home to Kennedy not only by some American officials here but by President Fernando Belaúnde-Terry and other Peruvians. Belaúnde has not publicized the aid cut, it is understood, for fear of fueling further anti-Americanism.

When asked about the situation at a students' meeting, Kennedy replied that he thought that the question of private investment was a matter for the Peruvians to decide on.

The Peruvian government is sponsoring the school project Kennedy visited as part of its Cooperación Popular program under which peasants develop their communities with a maximum of self-help, supplemented by public funds. Short of such funds, the government asked AID many months ago for about $15 million, mostly in machines, to help make Cooperación Popular a success in a reasonable amount of time.

So far, AID has ignored such requests, though its officials here have recommended that they be met in a reasonable degree.

AID funds for all purposes in Peru have been cut from $40 million in fiscal 1964 to $14 million in fiscal 1965, with the curve continuing downward. The holddown apparently affects only AID assistance and not funds coming from the Export-Import Bank, The Social Progress Trust Fund, and other sources of U.S. support.

PROFITS SPLIT ARGUED

The argument over oil revolves principally around the question of how profits should be shared. Standard Oil has indicated it might agree to a percentage split of 65-35 in Peru's favor as it has done in other parts of the world. Belaúnde, under pressure from leftists in his party, is holding out for an 85-15 split, which both Standard Oil and the U.S. Government feel is confiscatory.

An accord on Peru's terms, some U.S officials maintain, would, moreover, discourage further foreign investment in this country. And such investment is vi[r]tually needed, they stress, if the Alliance is to work.

Opponents of this say that whatever the United States may think about the need for foreign investment, economic pressure to force an investment agreement will simply add fuel to widespread charges of "American Imperialism" and help the Communists — now a small force in Peru.

It is pointed out that little or no economic pressure is exerted on some dictatorial and oligarchal regimes to push through social reforms under the Alliance for Progress.

Made in the USA
Las Vegas, NV
15 February 2022